FROM THE

OUTHOUSE

TO THE

MOUSE HOUSE

FROM THE
OUTHOUSE
TO THE
MOUSE
HOUSE

CRAP YOU NEED TO KNOW FOR A
DREAM-COME-TRUE CAREER

EVA STEORTZ

PELICAN PUBLISHING COMPANY
Gretna 2018

*The word "Pelican" and the depiction of a pelican are
trademarks of Pelican Publishing Company, Inc., and are
registered in the U.S. Patent and Trademark Office.*

Library of Congress Cataloging-in-Publication Data

Names: Steortz, Eva, author.
Title: From the outhouse to the Mouse House : crap you need to know for a
    dream-come-true career / by Eva Steortz.
Description: Gretna : Pelican Publishing Company, 2018.
Identifiers: LCCN 2017044144| ISBN 9781455623990 (hardcover : alk. paper) |
    ISBN 9781455624003 (ebook)
Subjects: LCSH: Career development--United States. | Job satisfaction--United
    States. | Walt Disney Company--Employees.
Classification: LCC HF5381.A2 S74 2018 | DDC 650.1--dc23 LC record available
at https://lccn.loc.gov/2017044144

Printed in Malaysia
Published by Pelican Publishing Company, Inc.
1000 Burmaster Street, Gretna, Louisiana 70053
www.pelicanpub.com

I am blessed with amazing friends and a very large supportive family, not all of whom can be thanked in a book intended to be short and sweet. To my husband Dennis, my son Nico, my mom Dixie, my brother David, and best friend Keri, plus everyone else who cheered me on while writing this book, I am forever grateful for the love and encouragement.

Most who know me would guess that this book is dedicated to my father, David Eugene Steortz. When I was in high school, he started bringing me articles about women succeeding in business and secrets to success tips from Dale Carnegie. Zig Ziglar's See You at the Top *was his favorite source material. Now here I am writing a career advice book some thirty years later. How could he have known so long ago my path would lead me here?*

My dad was a factory chemical operator to earn money for our family. We were his passion, but that job was not. Throughout his life, he was also a photographer, a retailer, and a real estate agent. He was forever chasing a dream. No matter what happened, he expected success was just around the corner. My father had unwavering positivity until his last day. Gratefully, it rubbed off on me. I found out that Pelican Publishing, the publisher of his well-used copy of See You at the Top, *was interested in publishing this book two weeks after my father passed. How incredibly serendipitous! Thank you for believing in me, Daddy. Your encouragement was the best gift ever and will always be my safety net. No mountain is too high to climb. I will see you again someday at the top.*

Contents

"Kid, you'll move mountains. Today is your day! Your mountain is waiting so get on your way."   —Dr. Seuss

●●●

"Never let your memories be greater than your dreams."   —Doug Ivester

●●●

"Time and balance: the two most difficult things to have control over yet they are both the things that we do control."   —Catherine Pulsifer

●●●

"It could be that those who dream more, do more."

—Stephen Leacock

Preface

West Virginia and California couldn't be farther apart or more different, and yet each of them is home to me. After college, I was fortunate to turn a one-way ticket west into a journey of a lifetime, ultimately achieving my dream-come-true career working for The Walt Disney Company for twenty years. It was sheer determination, some blue-collar grit, and a generally well thought out plan that got me there and allowed me to rise from Assistant Manager to Vice President in several Disney divisions.

Working at Disney was the best training in the world; like being at boot camp every day with other type A dreamers and doers. One gets to work with creative geniuses and legendary story tellers. It was the literal definition of working with a dream team. While not perfect, working at Disney was about as dream-come-true as a career can get.

Of course, life at the happiest place on earth isn't all pixie dust. It's a fifty-five billion dollar company, which makes it magical, *and* highly political. Serving the stock holders with increased revenue every year is the real mission as well as creating magic for families around the world. Expectations are high and change is rather constant. I survived many pixie dust storms, yet one day I did get laid off with hundreds of other talented people. It was the most disruptive and worst upheaval I ever witnessed involving a not-so-smooth integration of leaders after the purchase of Marvel.

A lot of super heroes were not victorious in this battle. Let's just say corporate politics can get uncomfortable and personal. When egos clash, it's more about leadership team survival than black and white practical business. Often, when your boss is out, suddenly you are out too. Choosing positivity over resentment, I decided to write this book celebrating all I learned from amazing leaders who motivated and inspired me to take risks and dream big. The process was therapeutic, transformative, and like living the lessons all over again.

It is my new mission to inspire others to aim high in their careers. I hope that by capturing and sharing my amazing training and experiences, others will be inspired to follow their dreams no matter where they are from or their circumstances. So here it is, the kind of real world plus inspiring and motivating book I wish I had read before diving head first into my career.

This book will unveil some unspoken truths about what you *can't control* in your career but the focus will be positive with tips in areas which you *can control*. Control the controllables is a major life lesson. Once you know them, the secrets are simple and straightforward. You won't find any intellectual pretenses here. You have likely heard some of these fundamental life lessons ever since you were young; maybe even within Disney animated movies where you are inspired to be kind, follow your dreams, and expect anything is possible. You will also likely recognize some of your favorite quotes in this book, as anchoring yourself with famous words of wisdom is always a good idea.

> To keep it simple, I call the secrets to career success your **RPM**s, the things you must do to keep moving forward. These are your Three Must Do's:
>
> - **R**ally your Relationships
> - **P**ossess Positive Style
> - **M**aster Self-Motivation

If you prioritize these three things that are fully in your control, you will absolutely enjoy a successful career. These are your *must do's*. That's right. It is all up to you! No more excuses. This book will help you retrench and recommit to what you set out to achieve and show you how to take control so you can start having more fun and progressing in your career now.

I was laid off at age fifty, and for me that's merely halftime. There are so many more mountains to climb and fun to be had. My hope is that I can inspire you while I continue to strive for pure fearlessness myself. Let's aim higher together.

Prologue

Once upon a time there was a little girl who sat in her grandmother's outhouse on a West Virginia mountain, door wide open, looking at the stars and dreaming of a big city career. Would I do it all again? *Yes.* But this time, even more *fearlessly* and with more *balance.*

If you are reading this, you have likely read (or at least have on your bookshelf) many other books on the topic of career success. Does the world really need another one? Well, maybe just this one more.

- One that doesn't try to be too text book-ish, but tells you straight up some stuff you need to know.

- One that concisely cuts to the chase and tells you *how* to manage your career growth by being a person everyone wants to work with, how to minimize your disappointments, and how to have fun along the way.

- One that uncovers some important nuances behind all the "secrets to success" the other books teach.

And maybe you want to hear it from someone who took a one-way ticket from West Virginia to California knowing nobody in the business, with no money, no job, no fancy degree but with deep determination and raw resolve to work in entertainment marketing in Hollywood.

After roles with CinemaScore, MGM, Young & Rubicam, twenty years at The Walt Disney Company, starting my own consulting company and now working for Twentieth Century Fox, I've seen a lot of crap. I have also learned some valuable, and often hard-core lessons in corporate politics, survival techniques, and the importance of defining your own success. I have enjoyed an exciting, prosperous, and fun career. I am excited to share some insights and strategies (a.k.a. some critical crap) many won't admit or take time to tell you. This book is filled with ideas on how to take every opportunity to learn, grow, and be true to yourself as well as prepare and deal with the all-too-common situations you can't control. It will also provide tips on how to focus on what you *can* control to ensure you have a thrilling, fulfilling, and successful career. Stories about some of my favorite memories and leaders will give you some strong practices. For further inspiration, I have added a lot of my favorite quotes. I start each day selecting a quote to inspire me and remind me of an important lesson. Self-motivation requires daily practice.

Confessions and Caveats

I have to admit while I worked really hard, I have also been really lucky. I got my first job at Disney via a classified advertisement in the *Los Angeles Times*. That was long before LinkedIn and before I had strong network and industry relationships that could have helped me. When I answered the ad, I knew it was a long shot but I went for it anyway and started visualizing myself with Mickey Mouse ears! While it might have been luck that I came across that ad, it was certainly guts that got me to place the call. Having crazy confidence and just being fearless can make a big difference in your success. I am going to give you some tips on getting into the company of your dreams with raw determination, using all the available resources and trying unique no-fear tactics.

Fearless maybe, but I am also an emotional, sentimental sucker. I cry at phone company commercials and, of course, Disney movies. Working at Disney was a dream-come-true for me. I really believed in wishing, dreaming, and magic. I loved and lived that brand. It's important to bring your heart to work. Your heart makes all the difference.

However, sometimes even when you do everything right, things still can go wrong. One day, two weeks before my twentieth anniversary with the Mouse, I got laid off. And it hurt. I actually felt my heart aching. Sure, I intellectually understood that it was just a job in a very large company with stockholder obligations, but for me it was personal. I really did start believing Disney was different; part of my family, not just a job. Choosing to still believe every fairy tale has a happy ending, I decided to be grateful for all I had learned and experienced and set out to seek my next adventure.

These are the crappy moments which give you time to pause, reflect, and reconnect with what you originally set out to do. I tried to remember the details of what I wanted to be when I was young. I actually visualized what the five-year-old me would say to the fifty-year-old me at that moment. And the answer was, of course, "aim even higher." From childhood until when I started college, I actually wanted to heal people. While trigonometry inhibited my ability to enter the health sciences, I had often thought over the years how cool it would be to help people overcome what holds them back so they go after their ultimate dreams.

So, believe it or not, it is true what they say, everything happens for a reason. You just have to pause and find the purpose. Everything is a gift we needed even if we didn't ask for it or even want it. *Everything* is an opportunity. Having a much-needed "summer vacation" gave me the time to take stock in my life progress, reconnect with my family, and refocus on my purpose. It also gave me time to write this book. While I successfully "survived" twenty years at Disney, writing this book helped me realize I would have done many things differently right up until the end. The break also helped me realize there were still a lot more exciting adventures and things I wanted to do and share with others in this creative life. So now, I am going to take my own advice and go forward with my eyes and my heart wide open, with clear intention and with an even healthier work and life balance.

Sometimes You Have to Go Back to Go Forward

Taking some time of reflection and going back home to West Virginia for some much-needed grounding gave me renewed courage. The answer "aim even higher" translated into a very happy and balanced new career as a marketing and career consultant. Getting clients and having success were largely due to rallying my relationships. Partnering with my dear ex-Disney friend, Brad Ong, and his marketing agency the Equinox Group, resulted in lots of exciting projects. Not only did we continue to work with many divisions of The Walt Disney Company, We supported teams at Nickelodeon, Universal, WarnerBros., DreamWorks, Mattel, Hasbro, and others. Having your own company gives you lots of control and flexibility. I got to spend my son's high school years able to make brownies for bake sales, attend his film class screenings, and take his friends to In-N-Out. I proactively made time to give back and especially loved helping young people find their confidence and build their plans to aim high in their careers.

And then just like that, a prior Disney leader landed a President position at Twentieth Century Fox and lured me back into the corporate world. I am now a Senior Vice President having a rather opposite-of-Disney experience working on adult targeted films and TV shows. I have gone from princesses to *The Predator* and I love it. I am sure Fox is going to be a whole new adventure yet I know my newest dream-come-true career is going to be helping others dream big and aim high! I don't exactly know what form it will take, yet I am very excited for the journey forward as we all find out. An important tip for all of you: even when you

> *"When one door shuts, another opens but we often look so long and regretfully upon the closed door we do not see the one which opens for us."*
> —Alexander Graham Bell

● ● ●

> *"Attitude is a little thing that makes a big difference."*
> —Winston Churchill

● ● ●

> *"Someday you will be old enough to start reading fairy tales again."*
> —C. S. Lewis

● ● ●

> *"Well behaved women rarely make history."*
> —Laurel Thatcher Ulrich

● ● ●

> *"There can be no happiness if the things we believe in are different than the things we do."*
> —Freya Stark

think you have achieved your dream job, leave a little room in your heart because, things can get even better.

So here is another confession. I love books but have a very short attention span. So, I wrote this book expecting many people have the same challenge in these fast-paced lives we lead. You can read this book pretty quickly, or in bite-sized chunks by skimming the headlines that interest you. There are seven simple exercises that can all be completed in one day, or you can select to do just the ones where you have immediate interests.

So just like luck presents you with opportunities, timing also plays a role. While I know ageism is a real thing, I choose to feel lucky to be starting fresh in my fifties in an era where other women have made fifty the new twenty-five. Madonna is still rocking and Michelle Obama is a charismatic, youthful mom. I arrived in Hollywood at age twenty-five ready to take on the world. At age fifty-five, I still believe the sky is the limit. Age is irrelevant. Don't let it, or anything else, be an excuse for you not to chase your ultimate dreams. Having a no-excuses attitude is another important secret.

Final Confession: My Style Is a Bit Saucy

I know the rules. Let's face it; a lot of them are crap. I rebel against many of them. I firmly believe you have to be true to yourself to really be successful and have some fun. Final confession: I can be a pretty wicked curser. Swearing is an area where I know the rules, but break them. You can imagine how popular this was at Disney. One of my favorite words is "sh--" which coincidentally fits very well, in fact literally, with my memories of dreaming in my grandmother's outhouse. I know it is not politically correct, but often this is the only word that will do the job. It is so amazingly versatile.

It was highly recommended I use "crap" as an alternative in this book as it is slightly more palatable. I agreed to the compromise, but just for the book, not in day to day practice. I did not agree with the many who recommended I not feature an outhouse on the book cover. After all, that is where the dream began and a very important part of the story.

I don't recommend breaking all the rules and ignoring the advice of others. However, I do recommend being true to yourself or your success will never feel authentic. The magic only works when you believe fully in the dream despite what others say is possible.

Relationships Are My Biggest Priority

People are fascinating. I love people and that has perhaps been my biggest asset. I am still in touch with people from all walks of my life including my childhood friends, college roommates, and many of my colleagues and bosses. Even before Facebook and LinkedIn, this was a major priority for me. Managing and enjoying the benefits of your relationships will always be a critical skill. This is one of the three main secrets. You need to excel at all of them—especially this one, though—to maximize your potential, as none of us can be successful alone.

What I Have Learned So Far

So here it is, brace yourself as I wish someone had told me this in a way I could have really grasped it at the start, or even middle, of my career.

We won't spend too much time on the work-related situations we can't control. Suffice it to say you need to be aware, you must show no fear, and you have to be ready for these volatile, often political "crap" storms as they are inevitable. Dig deep for your inner strength. You can survive, get stronger, and learn while you focus on controlling the controllables. Controlling what you can and letting go of the rest are the overriding secrets to being the architect of your own dream-come-true career.

In this book, I seek to simply summarize what I learned from some amazing bosses, and talented colleagues, as well as some work-related tactics and styles that worked well for them and for me along the way. I hope some of these "secrets to success" and the nuances I share provide direction and inspiration as you move forward in your career.

For the remainder of this book I am going to use headlines, bullet points, quotes, some short stories, and very simple but powerful exercises. Another "secret to success" is most people like it short, sweet, and simple. One of my favorite Disney corporate lessons is, "be brief, be bright, and be gone!" So, let's get into the short stories and lessons learned.

Chapter 1

The Corporate Truths: The Good, the Bad, and the Crappy

There are some truths you don't want to hear and that nobody wants to say aloud. This is a very positive and inspiring book, I promise. Don't worry, most of my career was amazing so most of this book is going to focus on the good. However, you need to know the truth: some elements of corporate America are kind of bad and sometimes it can be down-right crappy. So, we are going to get these things out of the way quickly and move on. Knowing and accepting these things are going to save you a lot of heartache. So here we go, here is some crap you need to know:

> **Justice does *not* exist (This crap ain't fair!)**
> **Hard work *does not* equal success (Are you sh--ing me?)**
> **Your job will *not* love you back (No crap!)**

The Crap You Can't Control—A Quick Summation
. . . Injustice

It is hard to understand "corporate politics." The phenomenon where a new leader comes in, fires everyone and brings in new people, often people less qualified, does not make practical business sense. However, it happens every day. Of course, the people "let go" have valuable experience and insights. Hard core lesson: we are all replaceable. When a change in business results or a shift in culture is desired, you will most often see a radical changeover of people. Nobody promised us that working for a corporation was going to be fair. Accept change as the only constant. See the potential in change and believe there will be new opportunities.

We have likely all seen the situation where someone with fewer qualifications gets a larger opportunity than they have earned. This is often based on prior relationships, a valued style, or maybe luck or timing. Don't let these situations anger you or make you question your self-worth. Learn from it, let it make you stronger, honestly assess what you could have done differently, and move forward with even more determination. Even when you are wronged, you *are* in control of how you respond to every situation.

"Blessed are the flexible for they are never bent out of shape."

—Michael McGriffy

• • •

"Thanks for the adventure. Now go and have a new one."

—Ellie, written in "My Adventure Book"
from the movie *UP*

• • •

"Each of us guards a gate of change that can only be opened from the inside."

—Marilyn Ferguson

• • •

"There are two primary choices in life. To accept conditions as they exist, or to accept responsibility for changing them."

—Denis Waitley

• • •

"The main thing is to be moved, to love, to hope, to tremble, to live."

—Auguste Rodin

• • •

"Look deep into nature and then you will understand everything better."

—Albert Einstein

• • •

"My favorite things in life don't cost any money. It's really clear that the most precious resource we have is time."

—Steve Jobs

• • •

"With an eye made quiet by the power of harmony, and the deep power of joy, we see into the life of things."

—William Wordsworth

. . . Long Hours

With my blue-collar blood, this trap has gotten me more than once. In many jobs, the work is never fully completed so there can be a tendency to strive for the impossible. Especially when you like your work, you may find yourself staying much later than your mind and body can tolerate. You may find yourself reading emails while important people in your life are talking to you. You may skip time with friends and family in favor of completing just one more task. You may skip lunch. You may try to rationalize that you cannot eat healthily or exercise as you simply have too much work to do. You will see many others doing this and you yourself will be tempted. Don't do it! I have never seen anyone get ahead by working all the time or even over time. It is not about how many hours you work, I guarantee you. Seek balance. Take care of your body. Enjoy your family, friends, and hobbies. Take time for the arts. Spend time with nature. Fuel yourself with fun and love and your work will be better quality. Your strong positive presence, your fresh ideas, your commitment to teamwork, and your strategic solutions are what will make a difference in your career. Not how many hours you can brag you worked in a week. Martyrs are not winners. There are not rewards for sacrificing all else in favor of work. You can love your work but know that it cannot love you. And here's another secret: love is why we are here. Prioritize well.

. . . Lack of Loyalty

Only humans and animals are capable of loyalty, not a corporation. Your relationship here is not unconditional or guaranteed for life and it is not always reciprocal. Don't leave yourself vulnerable for disappointment. Ensure you are getting what you need to feel balanced. Your company can and will leave you for no reason you can control. So enjoy the opportunity, learn, travel, get what you can, and grow. Give your best, but accept this fact and make abundant time for the people and animals in your life. You are in control of your heart and how you spread your love.

> "Until one has loved an animal, a part of one's soul remains unawakened."
> —Anatole France

> "Peace requires us to surrender to our illusions of control."
> —Jack Kornfield

Exercise #1
Identify Your Crappiest Challenge

● ● ●

Can you be truly honest with yourself? What is happening in your career? Are you killing it, or is it slowly killing you? What is your biggest obstacle, and therefore also your biggest opportunity to get back in control? Whether you are just embarking on your career, ready for a new one, or interested in getting ahead and having more fun in your present job, what is the crappiest thing standing in your way of success and joy? How will you change your response to it and get in control of your heart and direction?

The crappiest thing standing in my way of career happiness right now is ___
_____
_____.

I am going to get back in control of this crappy situation by starting to _____
_____
_____.

While I know it is up to me, I am going to reach out to _____
for support as I know I can't be successful all alone.

Chapter 2

Career Success Truths:
It's All About You

Are you ready for some straight up truth? I wish there were tricks of the trade and some magic tips that were foolproof. But it's just as you have heard, it really is all about you. Not your family, your parents, your boss, your Human Resources department, your degree, what school you went to, how smart you are, what you wear, and not even really about your unique skills. It is about who you are deep inside, what you really want, and how determined you are to have it! It's about your desire and your drive. You also need to be true to your core values as you define success and make your way forward in your career path. You must remain true to you. You must keep yourself accountable for aiming high and going after your wildest dreams. Sure, you will need support along the way, but you are the one who is in control of ultimately making your dreams reality.

Embrace Your History

. . . Be Proud of Where You Came From

First, let's take a moment to go back to the beginning. You need to acknowledge that where you come from matters. Your childhood molded you. You can't hide from it, bury it, or avoid it. Learn from any hurts, hardships, or failures you have endured. Treasure the memories of grandparents, holidays, vacations, and friends from school. Be grateful for all you have been given and know that people largely do their best. Forgive people who have disappointed you. Embrace everything you have experienced and let that experience, the good and the bad, be a part of your strength and power.

My dad worked in a chemical factory and my grandfathers were coal miners and loggers. That is *loggers*—people who cut down trees—not *lawyers* as my husband originally misheard within the southern accent of my family members he met. My mom and grandmothers were homemakers. And yes, I believe those can be the hardest careers of all. My mom kept our house spotless and our table filled all while looking beautiful. She put on lipstick to run the sweeper. Eva Mae, the grandmother from whom I got my name, has to be one of the strongest and most successful women in history. She raised eight children in a small house on a hill with no running water. She most often had a chaw in her cheek and some Wild Turkey in her hand. Nothing she had was new, but everything sure was clean. I don't know how many trips to the creek she made each day to keep the ringer washer going. I have fond memories of the smell of bleach and the sound of that humming motor.

Mamma Ricey was the proud leader of her West Virginia mountain and everyone knew it. In her late seventies, she shoveled her own snow, painted her own house wearing only a bra, and was the one everyone went to for advice regardless of the topic. Some called her "Sarge" as she was fully in charge. She laughed and moved forward no matter what happened to her along the way. She was grateful for her home, her family, and the vegetables she grew and canned. She is my role model and hero. It is her voice I hear when I have any doubts about what I can achieve. Her strength showed me to work hard and always *believe* in me. She defines positivity and success for me. The original Wonder Woman was from West Virginia.

Who Is Your Hero?

Who do you think of when you need inspiration or an extra push forward? Who wouldn't let you have any excuses? Who showed you what true grit looks like? It can be an accomplished athlete, a rags-to-riches celebrity, a selfless philanthropist, a humanitarian, or a family member who never let you down. Let this person be there for you in mind or body. What would they do in your place when you have a challenge? Listen, smile, breathe, and move ahead positively. You need never act alone. You have your hero and the anything-is-possible five-year-old you, always in your corner. They are always cheering you on.

Covet Your Secret Place

You know that meditation where you are asked to go to your secret place—the place where you feel most tranquil, and at peace? Most people choose a babbling brook or the ocean. Me? I go right back up that hill to my grandmother's outhouse. It was there I would sit with the door wide open, looking out at the lights on the mountains and the stars in the sky. It was there my dreams had the most clarity. I felt I could do anything. I felt lucky and excited to be alive. You may choose to file this under "weird crap" Eva shared. However, consider identifying with honesty the place where you first felt your purpose, centered in on a goal, and were inspired to aim high. Where did your dream begin? It's a good place to visit when you need a boost.

Who Are You? What Do You Want?

One of the most important things to remember and to lean on is the person you are deep inside. Your roots matter. This is your foundation, your strength, and your power. No matter where you came from, you and your heart and soul are what matters most. You need to define what success means for you with your inner compass as the largest guiding force.

"Thinking: the talking of the soul with itself."
—Plato

"Find joy in everything you do. Every job, relationship, home—it is up to you to love it —or change it."
—Chuck Palahniuk

"No one saves us but ourselves. No one can and no one may. We ourselves must walk the path."
—Buddha

"Hope is a waking dream."
—Aristotle

"Success means having the courage, the determination and the will to become the person you believe you were meant to be."
—George A. Sheehan

"Success is not so much what we have as it is what we are."
—Jim Rohn

"And that is when I heard the whisper in my heart's ear, it's not about your childhood, it's about who you are."
—C. Joybell C.

Exercise #2
My Past Determines My Future

● ● ●

When I was little I looked up to _____ and
I still aspire to be _____ like
them.

I always feel safe, energized, and most ready to conquer my dreams when I
take a moment to go deep into my mind and visit my secret place which is
_____
_____
_____.

I am proud of where I come from because _____
_____
_____.

My core values will drive my definition of success and what's most
important to me are _____
_____
_____.

FROM THE OUTHOUSE TO THE MOUSE HOUSE

Chapter 3
The Simple Secrets: Your Must Do's

So now you know it's all up to you, *but* what do you do? In short, you control the controllables and you take control. You focus on what you can do and you do those things with great focus and proactivity. Don't worry, it's a lot simpler than you think. In fact, magically simple. I have seen it in action my whole career. Here are the most important things you can do to thrive in your career and have a great time along the way.

Three Truths You Need to Accept: The Crap In Your Control Is What You Must Prioritize

Your Relationships matter more than your Skills.
Your Positive Style matters more than your Results.
Your Self-Motivation is your key to Success.

Prioritize Relationships

You have likely heard that "it's all about who you know" and sure, knowing the right people can be a great advantage. However, what if you don't know anybody? How do you know who you should know? And how exactly do you build and maintain relationships? We all have to start somewhere. Chapter 4 is full of ideas on this. And it is 1,000 percent true that knowing how to relate and work with people is way more important that your skills. Most anyone can learn a skill but not everyone knows it's all about prioritizing people. Here's another secret. Look around at work . . . people are the key to success and most of them are fun to hang out with professionally and personally.

Practice Positivity

Being positive no matter what is like knowing an important magic trick in your career. When you can see the lesson and opportunity in a situation and keep everyone focused on moving forward, you are well on your way to success. Think about it. Would you want to follow a leader who offers ideas and solutions or one who wants to focus on all that is wrong and whose fault everything is? This is a simple one but one very few people have mastered. Chapter 5 gives lots of examples and tips to support you in the very important pursuit of positivity.

Master Motivation

This may be the hardest area as many of us grew up believing that our parents, our teachers, and our bosses were supposed to support us and tell us what we needed to do to get ahead in life. It's not to say that we shouldn't seek their advice and support. We should. That is of course a big part of rallying our relationships. However, the real truth is, only you know what you want, what makes you happy and how high you wish to climb. We all want different things so there is not really one answer or a right answer to what makes one a success. Chapter 6 is designed to give you tips and inspiration to keep yourself inspired and motivated. Don't worry, it's ok if you don't know exactly where you want to go, just don't stop and by all means, do not ever go backward. You will find your way. RPM is designed to keep you moving forward.

Exercise #3
How Are My RPMs Today?

● ● ●

Relationships: My strongest allies and the people who I can count on to support my dreams are _____

_____.

Positivity: People tell me my greatest strengths and what makes me someone they want to be around is because I am always _____

_____

_____.

Motivation: When I am planning my next moves, I get myself organized and ready for action by _____

_____.

"There is nothing more truly artistic than to love people."

—Vincent Van Gogh

• • •

"No one in this world is pure and perfect, if you avoid people for their little mistakes, you will always be alone. So, judge less and love more."

—Jabez Richards

• • •

"Not all treasure is silver and gold, mate."

—Captain Jack Sparrow, from the movie
Pirates of the Caribbean: The Curse of the Black Pearl

• • •

"The key is not to prioritize what's on your schedule, but to schedule your priorities."

—Stephen Covey

• • •

"Our greatest fear should not be of failing, but of succeeding at things that don't really matter."

—Francis Chan

Chapter 4
Rally Your Relationships

Are you ready for some more rather surprising truths?

Your relationships are more important than your skills.
No one can be successful alone.
Your network is your lifeline, not how well you do your job.

Of all the intense work you have to do to drive your career, developing and maintaining your relationships can be the most fun and rewarding.

Prioritize People—At Home *and* At Work

Step away from your computer. Connect. **Engage.**
Ask for ideas and support. Reciprocate.
Relationships give life meaning.

Stay Connected
. . . Communicate

Call for no reason.
Get together and talk about everything and nothing.
Human connection is the key to everything.
It's the people you travel with that make the journey.

Hug Often
A hug is one of your greatest powers.
Be sure to pull them close; no air hugs allowed.

"No act of kindness, no matter how small, is ever wasted."
—Aesop

29

Share **Yourself with Others**

Be natural, fun, personable, playful, and cheerful.
Be authentic, but force yourself to be interested in others if you must.
Be giving; one nice gesture can make someone's day.
Share your light; be generous with your gifts.

"As we let our own light shine, we unconsciously give other people permission to do the same." —Nelson Mandela

• • •

"Be helpful. When you see a person without a smile, give them yours." —Zig Ziglar

• • •

"Success isn't just about what you accomplish in your life. It's about what you inspire others to do." —Unknown

Play **Hard**

There is no reason work cannot be fun! Lead by example.
Order pizza, play loud music, and be visible and smiling during crunch time.
Plan events to look forward to—team lunches, competitive shopping, or field trips.
Hard asses are lonely—the good guys are happier and win in the end!

"What then is the right way to live? Life should be lived as play." —Plato

• • •

"It is a happy talent to know how to play." —Ralph Waldo Emerson

They Call It Work for a Reason, but It Doesn't Have to Suck

I know I was lucky, but getting up and going to work was never a hardship for me. Work was fun largely because we made it fun. Projects were collaborative by design with teams of like-minded people tackling the next big ideas together. There was always the day-to-day, regular course of business work *plus* the game changers and you wanted to be on these new business "task forces."

Work itself should be fun in addition to the obligatory birthday celebrations, lunch outings, movie nights, happy hours, and whatever other fun adventures you can plan. One of my last "task forces" at Disney I called "Planning for Success." It was for the film *Brave* and positioning the main character, Merida, as a strong, empowered, alternative voice for girls. The goal was not to rely on the traditional tactics that made the princess brand so successful. The opportunity was to embrace an even more sporty, sassy, and take-charge character. Merida was the start of the empowering female trend. *Phew,* it was about time for more variety in the girls' toy aisle.

Be sure you are making work fun for you *and* for those around you. Develop some new big ideas that are true game changers and rally a team around you. Work hard, play hard, and ensure your efforts have purpose.

Show Your Gratitude to Others

Everyday express at least three things for which you are grateful.

Don't forget to say thank you to everyone; especially those who challenge you.

Take time to thank people for the big things and the small things they do for you.

Don't wait for birthdays and holidays to give thoughtful gifts; kind words count.

Shower your network of relationships with continuous gratitude, support, and love.

> "The only people with whom you should try and get even are those who have helped you." —John E. Southard
>
> "We must find time to stop and thank the people who make a difference in our lives." —John Kennedy

It's Never Too Late to Say Thank You

Lately, I have been reminiscing about all the people who were there at the big turning points in my life. Very spontaneously I sent an email to Ed, President of Cinema Score and the generous entrepreneur who gave me my first job in L.A. I had been sleeping on a friend's lumpy couch for three months, buying gas with found quarters, and not yet loving L.A. when I got his call. He took a big chance on me. I'll never forget how crazy and exciting it was polling people in Westwood theaters after movies. Forget being shy or timid when you are trying to get movie patrons to take a minute to answer your questions as they rush out of a theater.

I thanked him and let him know I always appreciated that opportunity, but never said it and just wanted him to know. Reconnecting meant a lot to both of us. I've sent a lot of these emails this year to play catch up. Going forward, I intend to do a better job of saying and showing my gratitude along the way. Who can you send a thank you e-mail to today? No excuses. Google and find them. Even small gestures mean a lot. Make someone else's day today.

Cherish Interesting Characters

Appreciate everyone you meet along the way.
Love even the loud and the unusual ones.
Love especially the ones that make you crazy.
Appreciate that everyone is different and yet the same.
Don't try to change people into the way you want them to be.
You may be surprised by which ones become your life-long friends.

"We all live with the objective of being happy; our lives are all different and yet the same." —Anne Frank

• • •

"Remember that everyone you meet is afraid of something, loves something, and has lost something." —H. Jackson Brown Jr.

• • •

"Most people need love and acceptance a lot more than they need advice." —Bob Goff

FROM THE OUTHOUSE TO THE MOUSE HOUSE

Whistle While You Work

One summer, while in college, I had the opportunity to work at my father's chemical plant insulating pipes. It paid well to support college tuition. Boy, did I dread this, my first real job was about as blue-collar gritty as it gets. Hard-hat, safety glasses and yes, I rocked the hard-toe work boot. Blue-collar summer was one of my favorites by far. The factory guys were so collaborative, supportive, and enthusiastic about their work. We had the greatest potluck lunches and what warm, colorful, interesting characters. I laughed all summer. No job is unbearable when you just let yourself enjoy the people around you. Make the most of *every* opportunity. Don't judge and don't make assumptions about people. Really get to know the people with whom you share eight or more hours a day. You will be pleasantly surprised by who you end up loving.

> *"Nothing is work unless you would rather be doing something else."*
> —James M. Barrie

Manage Up and Down and Sideways

Relationships are critical at all levels.
Remember the assistants know *everything.*
Ensure you have a strong "buzz" at all levels.
Network at least one level *above* your own.
Ask your peers what you can do better to support the team.
Ask for feedback from all levels and really listen and make changes.

Politics—You Have to Play to Win

Don't consider corporate politics dirty and as something to avoid.
Discover the power centers and get into those circles; at least visit them.
Consider "politics" a positive way for you to meet people, learn, and stretch.
Politics are often *how* you get things accomplished with due recognition.

Network—**The Best Ideas May Be Outside of Your Circle**

Ensure you are reaching out to people in different businesses.
Gather ideas and input from diverse perspectives.
Ask people outside your department about their success and ideas for you.

Why Didn't I Think of That?

Often the best ideas are the most obvious. You may be shocked by the staggering number of couples who have their wedding at a Disney theme park. Pam was a master at leveraging synergy and finding the next big idea. The bigger and bolder the better, and often those ideas were right under our noses. She collaborated with the Disney theme parks and launched the first line of high-end designer wedding dresses inspired by Disney Princesses. She also found ideas inside the legendary Disney vault and historical archives including replicating Walt's exact office furniture. Of course, Disney should license high-end leather chairs! Look around and talk to people. Your next big idea is likely a networking lunch away with someone new in a different department you never considered working with on a project. Look closely and you will see the next idea might be the most obvious—a why-haven't-we-ever-done-this-before "a-ha" moment.

"What we see depends mostly on what we look for."
—John Lubbock

Recruit the Best Talent

So long as they don't know it and show it; avoid the smart a--es and the dumb sh--s.
Hire people who complement your skills; expand the team's strengths.
Don't be afraid of people who know things you don't. Learn from them.

"Surround yourself with only people who are going to lift you higher."
—Oprah Winfrey

Hang Out with Other Superheroes

> *"It's time for us to stand and cheer for the doer, the achiever— the one who recognizes the challenges and does something about it."*
> —Vince Lombardi

Collaborate to Elevate

It's more fun and more effective to work as a team.
Two heads (or more) are truly better than one.

> *"Great things in business are never done by one person; they're done by a team of people."*
> —Steve Jobs
>
> *"When people work towards a common goal, they are driven, passionate, and purposeful."*
> —Richard Branson

Gather Multiple Perspectives

Assemble a diverse team (not people like you).
Insist on alternative points of view.
Develop a well-informed action plan.

Never Go It Alone; Share the Risks and the Rewards!

Assemble your superhero team!
Always use your contacts and network to expand upon your plans.
Use your relationships to plus up your ideas and evolve them.
Be sure you are giving more that you are receiving.
Ask for help and accept it graciously.
Supporting each other builds lifelong and meaningful human bonds.

> *"TEAM—Together Everyone Achieves More."*
> —Unknown

> *"Life doesn't make any sense without interdependence. We need each other and the sooner we learn that, the better for us all."*
> —Erik Erikson

> *"It is not so much our friends' help that helps us as the confidence of their help."*
> —Epicurus

Generosity of Spirit

Adopting our son was the best thing that ever happened to me but it was far from easy. Our legal complications were many, my heart was aching and bills were drowning us. My "work friends" provided great motivation and support. They also got together and organized a very impressive silent auction. I couldn't believe how many people donated items and showed up for a fun night of eating, drinking, and outbidding each other for crazy crap nobody needed. They raised $10,000 for us. Even more than the much-needed money, they raised our spirits and touched our hearts forever. Be there for people you work with and accept their support with gratitude.

Be Generous!

> *"You make a living by what you get, but you make a life by what you give."* —Unknown

> *"It is one of the most beautiful compensations in this life that no one can sincerely help another without helping themselves."* —Ralph Waldo Emerson

> *"If you get, give. If you learn, teach."* —Maya Angelou

> *"Those that bring sunshine to the life of others cannot keep it from themselves."* —J. M. Barrie

FROM THE OUTHOUSE TO THE MOUSE HOUSE

Let Your Friends Lift You Up!

No one can be successful alone.
Whatever idea you have will be better when shared.
Good day or bad: share it with friends.
No matter how successful you get, remember your childhood friends.

> "There's something about childhood friends that you just can't replace."
> —Lisa Whelchel

Step Away from Your Computer!

Practice old-fashioned face-to-face talking—resist sitting at your desk.
Suggest fifteen-minute coffee breaks to get to know people; everyone has fifteen minutes!
Ask people for their ideas, opinions, and support on your projects; it's for mutual benefit.
Recommend team outings; bonding over shared interests is invaluable.
Proactively build a diverse network of people you like, trust, and admire.
Build your professional network; you will likely also make some lifelong friends.

The Gift of Attention

There is no greater gift than giving someone your undivided attention. In the mid-nineties, the studios were still mostly a boys' club and being tough was celebrated as being in power. I imagine it was hard for our president, Anne, to stay so warm, kind, and friendly. Her greatest strength was her ability to make you feel important no matter what your level in the organization. She knew your name, or at least pretended to, with warm eyes and a smile. No matter how busy she was when you spoke to her, she looked right at you so you knew she was really listening.

So many of my bosses at the time barely took their eyes from their computer screens. With mobile phones, now it is even worse. Everyone is always looking down, racing to read one more email while running to the next meeting. We all do this. So much to do, so little time. I shudder remembering the times I did this to my son while working intensely for the Mouse. Step away from your desk and put down your communication devices when any other human honors you with their interest. Listen and offer your complete focus to the person standing in front of you. The ability to connect requires your undivided attention. There is no better use of your time.

> *"I've learned that people will forget what you said, people will forget what you did, but people will never forget how you made them feel."* —Maya Angelou

> *"One of the greatest gifts you can give someone is the gift of your attention."* —Jim Rohn

> *"Wherever we are, it is our friends who make our world."* —Henry Drummond

Friendships Matter Most. Be a Good Friend

Stay Connected

People's feelings are fragile.
Listen. Be kind. And accepting.
Be fully in the moment and present.
It's a great way to learn and the best way to bond.

> *"Spread love everywhere you go. Let no one ever come to you without leaving happier."* —Mother Teresa

● ● ●

> *"I get by with a little help from my friends."* —John Lennon

Relationship Secret—Always Bring Food!

> *"First we eat, then we do everything else."* —M. F. K. Fisher

Food Fuels Friendships

I always leave a bowl of peppermint patties on my desk to encourage drop by guests. Everyone from assistants to executive vice presidents would pop by, grab one, share a pleasantry and move on. Encouraging some company and quick breaks should always be a practice within collaborating teams.

During one particularly stressful tenure, I put out a large metal container filled with various salty, sweet, and highly caloric snacks. It was quickly dubbed "the trough" and we would all gather there when we needed a break or a boost. Another simple secret, if you put out food, friends will come.

Welcome to the Jungle

Conducting team retail store checks is common for many businesses. A group goes out to see their products first hand on store shelves and see how consumers are shopping the aisles and responding to your product. It is likely not common to cry on one of these store visits. I was in the Disney home video group when *The Lion King* came out on video for the first time. Our first stop was of course Walmart, the biggest retailer in the world. Standing at the front of the store, trying not to be obvious, a group of us anxiously waited to see what would happen as people entered the store and passed the gigantic video display. We did not expect the phenomenon which ensued. *Every* single shopper entering the store picked up one of those—now deemed huge and clunky—VHS tapes and put it in their shopping cart. There was no hesitation. There was no price checking. There was however lots of smiling. I feel lucky to have witnessed this and the team of us, which worked on this project are of course bonded for life. Go out and see firsthand how your work and what you do impacts people. Do it with people you want to know forever. Find the meaning in what you do.

Never Go Home Angry . . . Resolve Differences Quickly

We often spend more time with associates than our family, so the same rules apply.

Confront small differences swiftly before they have time to fester.

Talk openly and honestly about your intentions *and* your feelings.

Avoid gossip *and* never talk badly about anyone—no judging lest we be judged.

Be aware and acknowledge when someone opposes your view points—clear the air.

Ensure you are always on the same page.

It is ok to agree to disagree, but with due respect.

Strategically Disengage

Your heart and mind need complete breaks from work.

Refuel with family and friends guilt-free.

Vacations are not optional.

"You can disagree without being disagreeable." —Zig Ziglar

"Always let your conscience be your guide." —Blue Fairy, from the movie *Pinocchio*

"The art of living lies in a fine mingling of letting go and holding on." —Havelock Ellis

"Play is not luxury. Play is necessity." —Kay Redfield Jamison

"Happiness is living a life having fun, friends, and freedom." —Lorrin L. Lee

"Be true to your work, your word and your friends." —Henry David Thoreau

"The making of friends who are real friends is the best token of man's success in life." —Edward E. Hale

Mix Work and Play

Making a personal connection with people you work with closely is critical. First, it makes life more meaningful and fun. Second, it is good to have these close personal ties when crap goes wrong. You are going to want people to have your back. You are going to want to be able to talk openly and with candor. An easy way to connect is group lunches. Even when budgets are tight, you can always bring in food and do a picnic in the local park. When times are good, get more creative. When we were working on the Narnia movie franchise, a group of us learned how to fence. On the second movie, we learned how to ride horses. When we were working on *Pirates,* we learned how to sword fight. Not all of these were my ideas, but the drinks that followed always were. Wow, how much fun, and I am sure I will be lifelong friends with this team of people who shared my favorite career era. Suggest fun, relevant, and even crazy bonding ideas and create lifelong memories and friendships.

Meeting at the Pub

There is no work situation you cannot tackle together after sharing a pint, or three. Not to mention the often-resulting singing and dancing. I had a sales leader who could find the best pub in town no matter what city we were in—Kansas City to Las Vegas. He knew the importance of a team talking about life not just work. He chose to do it over beer but the principal can apply to any type of social gathering. His team was tight. Our collective results were impressive. My still lingering beer belly was well worth it, Bruce. Thanks for those memories and the forever friendship.

Creating a Creative Culture

Disney is a gigantic corporation, but at its heart is still a creative center. It is typical for sales, marketing, finance, and creative to behave like feuding beings from another planet at times. Understanding that we all once finger painted and created refrigerator masterpieces, Luis, head of creative for the consumer products division, insisted that everyone in the company have the opportunity to participate and show their creative ideas. He led a BIG IdEARS program where anyone in the company could pitch ideas with winning entries having the opportunity to present directly to the chairman. He provided blank Mickey head molds and encouraged everyone to paint one using their individual passions for a charity event. Providing fun and creative outlets and opportunities for people of all levels and from all departments to celebrate, contribute, and participate in the company's future is good business and a good way to solidify cross-department relationships. You will surely find that some of the most creative people are not necessarily in the creative department.

Be Like the Janitor

I am somewhat curious when managers brag they are "hands off." Delegating is important but too often hands off often means "I am the boss and don't really want to work." I always made sure any team I was on knew that I was *all* the way in no matter what was needed. I maintained my blue-collar ethics. One of my biggest pet peeves is when someone says, "That is not my job." That crap arches my back. Teamwork means you do whatever it takes and whatever you can to ensure success. Check in with your boss and your team members with a cheerful "Do you need any help?" and I guarantee that it will be music to people's ears. Your offer, if genuine, will solidify your relationships. Janitors do what needs done, no matter how dirty the job. Everybody knows the janitor. If you want to be popular, be like the janitor.

"We do not stop playing because we grow old; we grow old because we stop playing."
—George Bernard Shaw

"You can discover more about a person in an hour of play than a year of conversation."
—Plato

"The future belongs to the few of us still willing to get our hands dirty."
—Unknown

"Hard work doesn't guarantee success, but improves its chances."
—B. J. Gupta

"The best way to predict the future is to create it."
—Dr. Forrest C. Shaklee

Regrets, I've Had a Few

Regrets, mistakes, major screw-ups—whatever you call them, they are all part of the journey, and the goal is to learn as you go. I will tell you my biggest one and it's a real doozy. Please learn from this one. I buried its memory for a long time. I was even in denial for a while. My husband discovered a lump that turned out to be non-Hodgkin's lymphoma during a time when my work was particularly stressful. He asked me to take him to his first doctor's visit at City of Hope, at a specific date and time. Of course, it was exactly during a meeting where I wrongly thought my presence was critical. So, without thinking, I asked if he could change the appointment time. When he got upset, I truly did not understand. I was saying yes, just asking for a slight time adjustment. What a fool I was, and for a very long time. Don't check your work schedule when someone reaches out their hand to you, even if it's not a life-and-death scary time or not the person to whom you promised you would be there in sickness and in health. I hope you never do this to someone you love or even someone you like just a little. Prioritize people, especially your family. Period. No matter what.

Do the Right Thing—No Matter What

There will be pressures to cover up problems—don't.
There will be pressures to blame someone who does not deserve it—
    don't!
There will be times you could take credit for something you didn't do—
    don't!
There will be times you will be asked to let something unjust slide—
    don't!
Just don't do it. Do the right thing . . . no matter what!

> *"Ability may get you to the top, but it takes character to keep you there."*
> —John Wooden

> *"You are the hero of your own story."* —Joseph Campbell

> *"At any given moment, you have the power to say, 'this is not how the story is going to end.'"* —Christine Mason Miller

> *"Sometimes the right path is not the easiest one."*
> —Grandmother Willow, from the movie *Pocahontas*

Be a Pearl Hunter

Developing relationships within your work environment includes engaging at all levels. Relationships are important with your peers, your management team, and those who work for you. At a leadership retreat, many were asked to present their idea of what makes a good leader. One of the most memorable stories focused on the importance of a leader being a pearl hunter. The brilliant message was that a leader's role is to find the gem within each person. Everyone had a gift to share and a leader's role is to find it and let that person shine. I always think of that story when someone is struggling with an employee or even a boss. You have to believe that everyone has a special talent or skill to share. We can be too quick to judge people harshly. People are worth the time even if we have to hunt a bit. You will likely find a talent that needs developed. Maybe you help someone find a talent the person doesn't yet know they possess. Maybe you find that a person's talent is better served in a different role they never considered. The real message is about giving everyone a chance. As leaders, and as people working with other people, as Francesco so beautifully articulated, let's all be pearl hunters.

On with the Show

Rarely has the departure of an executive resulted in as much emotional anguish as that of Dick. He was a thirty-two-year Disney veteran who worked his way up from running the train at Disneyland to running the entire studio. As chairman, he had a magical spring in his step and a passionate sparkle in his eyes. Disney pixie dust practically swirled around him as he walked the halls. He wasn't Texan, but I always imagined him wearing a very large white hat. He is one of the good guys. A gentlemanly showman full of positive energy and charisma in everything he did. He prioritized relationships with other executives, with actors, directors, and with friends. Despite his many years and contributions, Dick was asked to leave his beloved company. Remember the crap we can't control. Things are often not fair. We are all still cheering for you, Dick. The stars are in your favor and the next stage will be your own. A whole new world awaits you.

Exercise #4
Rally Your Relationships

● ● ●

Building and maintaining relationships is some of the most important work you must do. The steps to establishing and maintaining close and meaningful relationships can be straightforward and simple. To fully maximize this opportunity, you have to commit to regular efforts however and if this is not one of your focuses, you must start now. This week, and every week thereafter, here are three important tasks to add to your Must Do List.

1) Call someone and thank them for the support they have provided you (note: you can go back as far as you like including teachers, first bosses, mentors, etc.).

This week, I am going to thank _____.

2) Reach out and offer your support to someone you know needs assistance you can easily provide. Be generous.

This week, I am going to offer my support to _____

3) Ask someone for advice, ideas, resources, or even funding for a project in which you need support. Expect generosity. People love to help each other.

This week, I am going seek advice and support from _____.

By proactively reaching out and engaging with your network on an ongoing basis, you are nourishing it. Keeping your relationships healthy is also fun. Make people a top priority.

"Think of the happiest things, it's the same as having wings."
—Peter Pan, from the movie *Peter Pan*

● ● ●

"Few things in the world are more powerful than a positive push. A smile. A word of optimism and hope."
—Richard M. Devos

● ● ●

"When you are totally at peace with yourself, nothing can shake you."
—Deepam Chatterjee

● ● ●

"A pessimist sees only the dark side of the clouds and mopes; a philosopher sees both sides and shrugs; an optimist doesn't see the clouds at all as he is walking on them."
—Leonard Louis Levinson

● ● ●

"First, they ignore you, then they ridicule you, then they fight you and then you win."
—Gandhi

● ● ●

"Anything worth having is worth fighting for."
—Thomas Jefferson

● ● ●

"You don't always win your battles but it's good to know you fought."
—John Greenleaf Whittier

● ● ●

"Somewhere something incredible is waiting to be known."
—Carl Sagan

Chapter 5

Possessing Positive Style: Create Your Future, Define Your Style

It's All in Your Presence; Your Personal Style and Being Positive No Matter What

Let's talk about presence and how your personal style matters more than results. This is the first truth few will tell you in your career. I have seen many managers with double-digit sales increases get fired because their "style" did not "fit" an organization. No matter their skills or results, people get fired who are deemed too aggressive, too non-collaborative, too arrogant, etc. I have seen this dismissal happen at every level in an organization from top to bottom: assistant to chairman.

Your style matters and maintaining positivity is the secret. So, how do you want to show up? What do you want people to say about you when you are not in the room? What do you want your "buzz" to be? People talk about each other *a lot* so harness this as a major opportunity.

There is much written about the importance of branding yourself. It is a lot simpler than many make it. You can define your presence proactively, be true to it and be consistent. It is as simple as using your words. Define the best you. The person you wanted to be when you were five. The person you still want to be. And it should not be all corporate buzzwords. We need to prioritize our human core values. We should be bringing our heart to the work place, not just a desire to get ahead.

> *"It takes courage to grow up and become who we really are."*
> —E. E. Cummings

Exercise #5
DEFINING YOUR STYLE USING YOUR WORDS

● ● ●

So, let's go ahead and do this simple yet significant exercise as an important step in defining your winning style and proactively plan your professional presence. Remember how our parents always told us to use our words? That advice is still fully applicable.

Simply choose three self-defining words and consistently show up that way no matter what! Use these words to describe yourself and others will begin to talk about you the way you want to be known. It is as simple as defining yourself and remembering to use your words no matter what situation you find yourself in. Simply become the most X, X, and X person you have ever known. Hold yourself accountable. Every day is an opportunity to be the best you.

Here is a list of style-oriented attributes to help you get started:

Determined	Creative
Unstoppable	Good Listening
Loving	Strategic
Reliable	Generous
Ambitious	Rule Challenging
Joyful	Funny
Kind	Graceful
Loyal	Charismatic
Game Changing	Supportive
Collaborative	Communicative
Problem Solving	Innovative
Daring	Calm
Confident	Motivating
Committed	Curious
Bold	Expressive

I am committed to showing up consistently as the most_____, _____, and _____ person you are ever going to meet. Welcome to your new mantra. You are sure to shine.

FROM THE OUTHOUSE TO THE MOUSE HOUSE

> *"The most creative act you will ever undertake is the act of creating yourself."*
> —Deepak Chopra
>
> *"Become the most positive, enthusiastic, and determined person you know."*
> —Zig Ziglar
>
> *"Make every day your masterpiece."*
> —John Wooden
>
> *"Life isn't about finding yourself. Life is about creating yourself."*
> —George Bernard Shaw
>
> *"Be yourself. Everyone else is taken."*
> —Oscar Wilde

The Truth: Your Positive Style *Matters* Even More than Your Results

Remember we are not talking about your wardrobe choices. Your style is how people perceive your leadership presence. There are a lot of pointers to follow with absolutely the most critical one being: be positive no matter what. Here are tips, in no particular order, on how you can exhibit a winning style and become someone everybody champions, cheers on, and wants to work with:

Harness the Power of Positivity

Be positive, no matter what.
In chaos or crisis, be the first to point out the lesson and the next move.
Be the lone voice that won't stop or accept defeat.
Say "yes" often. People don't like the word "no."
It is ok to follow "yes" with caveats like "and here are my recommendations."
When you do feel negative—retreat, recharge, and reemerge with solutions.

> *"Live life as if everything is rigged in your favor."*
> —Rumi

> "The mind is everything. What you think you become."   —Buddha
>
> "Pessimism leads to weakness, optimism to power."
> —William James
>
> "If you can't say something nice, don't say nothing at all."
> —Thumper, from the movie *Bambi*
>
> "Life is ten percent what happens to us, and ninety percent how we respond to it."
> —Lou Holtz

Do Not Avoid Conflict

Walk into the storms with confidence.
Stay calm. Find solutions. Lead others through.
Lead like a hero. Fight for what is right.

> *"Stay strong during the down times as it's all part of the ride."*
> —Eva Steortz

Candid Confrontation

In twenty years, there are only a few times I recall where I had significant conflict. It's not uncommon to disagree at work and usually it's pretty easy to find compromise through civil conversation. We all have our hot buttons. One of mine is email.

This happened once and I considered my most positive response before blasting off an equally emotional email to one I received. Work should rarely be about emotions. I just got up from my desk and walked straight into the emailer's office and said something like, "What is this really about as I am sure we can work it out?" Turns out there was a lot of unnecessary frustration and worry and a need to clarify the differences between our roles and responsibilities. Try and work out your differences face to face before small matters become potential relationship problems. Remember the people matter most.

"The best way out, is always through."   —Robert Frost

● ● ●

"Anyone can hide. Facing up to things, working them through; that's what makes you strong."   —Sarah Dessen

● ● ●

"Not everything that is faced can be changed, but nothing can be changed until it is faced."   —James Baldwin

Know When to Move Forward Positively but Change Course

Don't be a cheerleader on the *Titanic*.
Note that your best attribute in excess can also be your weakness.
Be honest. Be vocal when it is time to retrench, reduce resources, or restrategize.
Use fact-based recommendations; provide clear directions.
(Important Note: providing *solutions* is the secret to being *"strategic"*)

"If you want light to come into your life, you need to stand where it is shining."   —Guy Finley

● ● ●

"Those who move forward with a happy spirit will find that things always work out."   —Gordon B. Hinkley

Remain Confident

Never let them see you sweat.
Do research and garner lots of advice when you don't know the answers.
Give credit to those who supported you while standing tall for the applause.

"I am not afraid of storms for I am learning how to sail my ship."
—Louisa May Alcott

● ● ●

"With confidence, you have won before you started."
—Marcus Garvey

● ● ●

"I have great faith in fools, self-confidence my friends call it."
—Edgar Allan Poe

● ● ●

"You are very powerful provided you know how powerful you are."
—Yogi Bhajan

Never, Never, Never Complain

Do not bring up a problem, unless you have a solution.
Do not point out an issue, unless you have a recommendation.
Do not criticize, unless you have a constructive idea for improvement.

"A problem is a chance for us to do our best." —Duke Ellington

Advocate Sticking Together No Matter What

Champion what is best for all.
Be a "we-are-all-in-this-together" leader.
Don't ever go it alone, unless you want to be alone.

"Success comes when people act together; failure tends to happen alone."
—Deepak Chopra

Smile and Connect

This seems obvious but many don't do it. Such a simple yet powerful secret:
Look people in the eye and smile—even stronger!
Focus and be present when around others.

> *"Every day is a gift. Make the most of your present."* —Eva Steortz

> *"A smile is the shortest distance between two people."* —Victor Borge

Laugh Often

Laugh because you are having fun.
Laugh to bring levity to an absurd situation.
Laugh when you are right *and* when you are wrong.
Laugh often and with great intensity—even if you snort.

> *"Give up being right. Instead radiate harmony, peace, and laughter from your heart."* —Deepak Chopra
>
> *"A laugh can be a very powerful thing. Why sometimes in life it's the only weapon we have."* —Roger Rabbit, from the movie *Who Framed Roger Rabbit?*
>
> *"The most wasted of all days is one without laughter."* —E. E. Cummings

Keep Your Childhood Spirit

Stay five years old.
Having fun is allowed and encouraged.
Stay silly. Make lots of time to play.
Remember when you believed in magic; do that again!
Know we are all just big kids so laugh and have fun.

Work Hard. Play Often. Rest as Needed

> *"Life isn't as serious as the mind makes it out to be."* —Eckhart Tolle
>
> *"The most potent muse of all is our own inner child."* —Stephen Nachmanovitch

Possessing Positive Style

Enjoy the Perks

Don't feel guilty having fun with coworkers.
Take full advantage of whatever product, service, or benefit your company offers.
Share the perks. One man's job may be another man's dream.

> *"No man is a failure who is enjoying life."* —William Feather

The Power of Positivity

Vince could light up a room. Everything would stop, and people of all ranks would literally call out his name and often applaud when he entered a room. "Yeah! Vince is here!" He was positive no matter what. The worst thing anyone ever said about Vince was he couldn't carry a tune but he sang anyway. He smiled, laughed, and often belted out show tunes while walking up and down the halls. *There's no business, like show business* being his favorite. Everybody wanted him at their meetings. Everybody cheered his success. Everybody defended him if anything went astray. He had a positive idea to combat any challenge. He would look you in the eye, smile and say, "We are still having fun aren't we—how bad can it be?" He had a winning style. He was positive no matter what. His business grew double digits. He had the most positive of combinations. He became a senior vice president at Disney before he was forty and his own toy company at forty-five. Before fifty, he became a president of marketing at Universal Studios. Yeah Vince! We are still cheering despite your incredibly bad singing.

> *"Always believe that something wonderful is about to happen."*
>
> —Sukhraj Dhillon

Be Charismatic. It's Enthusiasm on Steroids

Everything depends on energy. Be sure yours is high!
Let your visions of all that is possible fuel you and others.

> *"Enthusiasm moves the world."*
>
> —Arthur Balfour

Be Passionate

Life is your stage.
Give your best performance every day.
Believe in yourself. Believe in all you do.
Go for it with great gusto.

> *"Desire! That's the one secret in a career. Not education. Not being born with hidden talents. Desire."*
>
> —Johnny Carson

> *"Don't ask yourself what the world needs. Ask yourself what makes you come alive and go do that, because what the world needs is people who have come alive."*
>
> —Howard Thurman

Be Show-Worthy

Consider everything you do to be your show.
Practice, set the stage, and own the spotlight.
Exceed expectations no matter what your task.
Earn praise for whatever role you get as you work your
   way up!

> *"Go confidently in the direction of your dreams! Live the life you have imagined."*
>
> —Henry David Thoreau

Strive for Excellence!

"We are what we repeatedly do. Excellence therefore is not an act but a habit."
—Aristotle

"The will to win, the desire to succeed, the urge to reach your full potential, these are the keys that will unlock the door to personal excellence."
—Confucius

"Whatever you are, be a good one."
—Abraham Lincoln

Be Open-Minded

Consider anything possible.
Be delighted by your potential.
Explore with curiosity, just like when you were five.

Ready. Set. Go for It!

You have to act, not just speak.
Dream, goal, plan, then take action.
Follow through is critical.

"You can't build a reputation on what you are going to do."
—Confucius

Have a Memorable Mission

Jim always had a clever tagline for everything. Under his leadership, we were to focus on "The three Cs"—communication, collaboration, and creativity. He never wavered from this mantra during his town hall presentations or his walks through the halls. His clarity and enthusiasm for his mission were contagious. His mission statement while he led the Disney Stores was also brilliant: "Be the best fifteen minutes of a child's day." He also hosted "Java with Jim," inviting team members of all levels to coffee for informal chats. I must thank him for his fourth C—charisma. His energy was always on high. His ability to connect with a crowd and get them cheering so impressive. His leadership is legendary. I feel lucky to have enjoyed it then and again now.

Leadership—Simply Defined

> *"A leader is one who knows the way, goes the way, and shows the way."*
> —John Maxwell

> *"Managers light a fire under people. Leaders light a fire in people."*
> —Kathy Austin

Be Unique—Live a Colorful Life

Have role models, but don't model yourself after anybody.
Focus on what makes you different.
Embrace your given gifts.
Let others be a part of your world.

Cue the Confetti Cannon

Never was anyone in a more perfect role based on their skills than Dan. He led the Events Team which was as surreal as Dan's whole life, which was pretty much a spectacular event. He was famous for over-the-top balloon installations, somewhat risqué live entertainment and of course, each presentation had to end with a musical performance and a confetti cannon. Many didn't realize that Dan's father passed early in life, making Dan fully committed to making the most of every single day and every single experience.

Once we were on a business trip together in Kansas where I expected we would have an early dinner and a relaxing, though somewhat boring evening. No. That was not in the cards. Somehow Dan found a stretch limo that took us to a casino on the water where we gambled into the wee hours. Dan resigned from Disney to start his own theater production company and has had many successful shows on Broadway. His show goes on and in glorious standing ovation style. Bravo Dan!

> *"The more you like yourself, the less you are like anyone else, which makes you unique."*
> —Walt Disney

> *"Why fit in when you were born to stand out?"*
> —Dr. Seuss

> *"Whenever you find yourself on the side of the majority, it's time to pause and reflect."*
> —Mark Twain

> *"In order to be irreplaceable one must always be different."*
> —Coco Chanel

> *"They are going to stare. Make it worth their while."*
> —Harry Winston

> *"You've got to dance like there's nobody watching"*
> —William W. Purkey

Stay True to You

Listen to input, but edit.
Follow your instincts.
Do what feels right to you.

> *"To be yourself in a world that is constantly trying to make you something else is the greatest accomplishment."*
> —Ralph Waldo Emerson

Being Vulnerable Takes Courage

Reveal the real you to people.
Be strong, yet transparent.
Be ambitious, yet grateful.
Be confident, yet humble.

> *"You can't get to courage without walking through vulnerability."*
> —Brené Brown

> *"Vulnerability is the birthplace of innovation, creativity, and change."*
> —Brené Brown

Be Innovative

Identify new opportunities.
Send a new idea around for input and offer to lead the effort.
Suggest something new—never done is the most fun.
Push a good idea even higher.
Research best practices in other industries and find translation to yours.

> *"Don't think 'what's the cheapest way I could do it,' or 'what's the fastest way I could do it,' think 'what's the most amazing way I could do it.'"*
> —Richard Branson

Be Creative!

> *"Creativity is intelligence having fun."*
> —Albert Einstein

> *"Every child is an artist. The problem is how to remain an artist once we grow up."*
> —Pablo Picasso

Mandatory Evolution

When you are at the top of your game it is easy to get comfortable and keep repeating what led you to success. Rich would not stand for that. In every new Disney Channel show marketing plan, he demanded at least one idea that had never been done before by anybody. It got to the point that all pitches to him included a "first time ever" icon burst kind of like the "As seen on TV" or "New and Improved" ones you see on products. I learned a lot from this demanding leader and I adopted that brilliant idea immediately. Try it with your team. Ask "What can we do we have never done before?" People will squirm at first. This is a secret for both fun and progress. Push yourselves and others to try new things, take risks, and of course aim high!

> *"It's kind of fun to do the impossible."*
> —Walt Disney

> *"Do something today that your future self will thank you for."*
> —Sean Patrick Flanery

> "You get in life what you have the courage to ask for."
> —Nancy Solomon
>
> "Breakthrough requires stretch and challenge." —Peter Fisk
>
> "Those who don't believe in magic will never find it." —Roald Dahl

Try New Ideas

> "The value of an idea lies in the using of it." —Thomas Edison
>
> "A ship in harbor is safe, but that is not what ships are built for."
> —John A. Shedd

Rules Are Merely Guidelines

Rules often need some challenging.
Acknowledge the rules while breaking them.
Rewrite the rules following each success. Taking risks can be transformative.

Breaking the Rules of the Kingdom

Disney story telling rules are very sacred and often quite literal. The characters all come from very specific and unique fairy tale worlds and these worlds must be kept separate and maintained with consistency. There was a time when it was strictly prohibited for the Princesses to appear together as they each came from different stories and kingdoms. There are many corporate stories about the origin of the now $4 billion Disney Princess brand. The true one is that someone at the Disney Stores broke the rules knowingly and developed a t-shirt featuring several of the Princesses in a group pose. Sales were so strong that the success was celebrated despite the well-known brand management rule. So now the Princesses live happily ever after together in most five-year-old girls' toy boxes and closets. While now up to five Disney Princesses can be featured together on a product, there are additional rules that are so secret I cannot tell you about them. True story. Seriously.

Take Charge

Someone has to lead, why not you?
Schedule meetings to discuss opportunities.
Persuade others to see new possibilities.
Suggest brainstorms; lead brainstorms to find solutions.
Recruit allies and lead them forward.
Train your allies, trust them, and unleash them.

> *"Ideas are the beginning points of all fortunes."* —Napoleon Hill

Be Innovative

> *"Do not go where the path may lead, go instead where there is no path and leave a trail."* —Ralph Waldo Emerson
>
> *"The best way to have a good idea is to have a lot of them."* —Linus Pauling

Plan for Success and Define What It Looks Like

State a big goal and be its loyal unwavering ambassador.
Define what success looks like and promote it—say it out loud to everyone!
State your goals enthusiastically, firmly, and keep moving forward.
Listen, learn, and refine—but never stop moving forward!
Name your projects and teams; promote them like a rock band!

Say It Out Loud

While in college working on my thesis, I remember saying to my teachers and classmates, "I am going to move to Hollywood and work in Product Placement in the movie business." They doubted. Laughed. Rolled their eyes in fact. When we were working on the sequel to *Pirates of the Caribbean*, everyone was documenting all the reasons why it would never become a major merchandising success. I said, "We can build this into a billion dollar business." They laughed and doubted too. Didn't really phase me except to maybe make me even more determined to succeed. I always liked the challenges. The victories feel so much sweeter when you have done what others deemed impossible. We all know the advice about the law of positive attraction and

Possessing Positive Style

believing it so much that you just make it happen. Well, I am here to tell you that that crap works. I don't have my pony yet, but I know I will someday when the time is right. State your goals firmly, confidently, and out loud. Put it out there to the universe. Commit to it yourself, hold yourself accountable, and get people rallying around you and offering their support. And then go for it with all you got. It is up to you to make it happen. Say it out loud, believe it, take action, accept help and don't stop until you get there!

"Tell me what it is you plan to do with your one wild and precious life."
—Mary Oliver

● ● ●

"Setting goals takes desire. Completing them takes determination."
—Ron Hawks

● ● ●

"A goal is a dream with a deadline."
—Napoleon Hill

● ● ●

"At the center of your being, you have the answer: you know who you are and you know what you want."
—Lao Tzu

● ● ●

"There can be no happiness if the things we believe in are different than the things we do."
—Freya Stark

● ● ●

"Take time to deliberate, but when the time for action has arrived, stop thinking and go in."
—Andrew Jackson

● ● ●

"Some succeed because they are destined to but most succeed because they are determined to."
—Henry Van Dyke

Dream Big!

"If you have built your castles in the air they are where they should be. Now put the foundation under them."
—Henry David Thoreau

• • •

"Let your dreams be bigger than your fears and your actions louder than your words."
—Zig Ziglar

• • •

"I want to put my ding in the universe."
—Steve Jobs

• • •

"The world needs dreamers and the world needs doers. But most of all, the world needs dreamers who do."
—Sarah Ban Breathnach

• • •

"In order to attain the impossible, one must attempt the absurd."
—Miguel de Cervantes

Be New and Improved Every Year!

Be sure you stay true to the words you want to be known for: "creative," "strategic," etc.

But be sure you are also always refining and seeking ways to up your game.

Be consistent but innovate and add new talent and skills.

Reinvent yourself—stay relevant, know the trends; adopt some of them.

"Be patient with yourself. Self-growth is tender: it's holy ground. There is no greater investment."
—Stephen Covey

"As you reinvent your life endlessly, you should open your minds to the infinite possibilities that do exist."
—Steven Redhead

Read. **Always Seek to Learn**

"There is more treasure in books than in all the pirates' loot on Treasure Island."
—Walt Disney

"Leave some room in your heart for the unimaginable."
—Mary Oliver

"It's what you learn when you know it all that counts."
—John Wooden

Be Confident

Keep your head held high; walk with purpose.
Make eye contact and speak with strong intent.
Focus. Fear nothing.
Introduce yourself to everyone at all levels.
If you don't have the answer—be the first to say you will go find it!

"The world makes way for the man who knows where he is going."
—Ralph Waldo Emerson

"Whether you think you can, or you can't, you are right."
—Henry Ford

Love the Work

"Opportunity is missed by most people because it is dressed in overalls and looks like work."
—Thomas Edison

Practice and Be Prepared

"The future depends on what you do in the present."   —Gandhi

"Opportunity dances with those already on the dance floor."
—H. Jackson Brown, Jr.

Never Let Them See You Sweat

Be prepared. Walk into a room organized and ready. (I put on lipstick and smile.)
Be ready for a daily dose of drama—and be a role model on how to respond.

> *"Fortune favors the prepared."* —Louis Pasteur

Be Slow to Panic

Move quickly to the solutions; promote the positive potential.
Never be combative.
Be grateful to those who challenge you to be better.
Use humor, charm, or whatever you own to keep control of any situation.

> *"Have a heart that never hardens, a temper that never tires and a touch that never hurts."* —Charles Dickens

Worry Less

Pick something and just take action.
Prioritize well and let the rest go.
Give yourself a break.

> *"Worry is a misuse of the imagination."* —Dan Zandra

Learn and Move On

Of course you are going to make mistakes.
Don't be too hard on yourself; you took a chance.
Of course bad things beyond your control are going to happen.
Find the lesson even if it is that things don't always make sense so be flexible.

> *"If you stumble, make it part of the dance."* —Unknown
>
> *"Every experience, no matter how bad it seems, holds within it a blessing of some kind. The goal is to find it."* —Buddha

Possessing Positive Style

> "As long as the world is turning and spinning, we're going to be dizzy and we're going to make mistakes." —Mel Brooks

> "Failure is the condiment that gives success its flavor." —Truman Capote

> "Remember there are no mistakes, only lessons. Love yourself, trust your choices, and everything is possible." —Cherie Carter Scott

> "When you come out of the storm you won't be the same person that walked in. That is what the storm is all about." —Haruki Murakami

Quiet Confidence

Our CFO Anne was the epitome of grace under fire. A true face of calm in any storm. Her mind was always working even if she sat in quiet observation. Her words carried great weight, as they were carefully chosen, direct, firm, and yet warm. She could detect an error in an Excel spreadsheet at twenty paces. Her ability to use numbers to make an inarguable point was beyond impressive. Strong, successful women can be kind, soft spoken, and generous yet full throttle, always-in-control powerhouses. Quiet doesn't always work in leadership, but when you back it up like Anne does, watch out world.

> "Silence is a source of great strength." —Lao Tzu

Be Keenly Self Aware

Seek perspective not perfection.
Laugh with yourself.
Laugh at yourself.
Be a humble work in progress.

> "Oh, happy the soul that saw its own faults." —Rumi

> *"Blessed is he who has learned to laugh at himself for he shall never cease to be entertained."*
> —John Boswell

> *"We don't see things as they are, we see things as we are."*
> —Anais Nin

Communicate Well

KISS: *Keep it Simple Stupid* is only part of the solution.
Simple is critical and so is smart and strategic.
Ensure your communication uses strong facts and rationale.
Make it sexy too. Add some flair.
Have a memorable headline and summary.

> *"Knowledge is the process of piling up facts; wisdom lies in their simplification."*
> —Martin H. Fischer

> *"Life is amazingly good when it's simple and amazingly simple when it is good."*
> —Terri Guillemets

> *"Life is really simple, but we insist on making it complicated."*
> —Confucius

Pictures Speak a Thousand Words

Use visuals and graphs with as few words as possible.
Make your points easy to grasp with headlines, bullet points and
visuals.
Bucket information into threes—simple equals memorable too.

> *"Of all our inventions for mass communication, pictures still speak the most universally understood language."* —Walt Disney

> *"I have just three things to teach: simplicity, patience, and compassion. These are your greatest treasures."*
> —Lao Tzu

Communication Takes a Lot More than Words

Strong communication includes action.
Demonstrate your intentions.
Walk your talk.

Be Bright, Be Brief, and Be Gone

Leave them wanting more!
Tell them only what they need to know.
Include an addendum to show your impressive homework.
Less is more. Force everything into easy-to-read one page formats.

Be Prepared

Raise your hand and volunteer for opportunities.
Stay connected and know leadership's priorities.
Be ready when opportunity calls or gives you a hard knock.

> "Luck is what happens when preparation meets opportunity."
> —Lucius Seneca

Ensuring Readiness

Do your homework; ask for input, get more input than you need.
Get initial feedback from stakeholders (test drive your ideas).
Build alliances; be sure others are going to back you up.
Anticipate objections and consider potential barriers.
Imagine it going perfectly yet anticipate what could go wrong.
Sweat the details—do you have your power cord and the tech support
    lined up?
Rehearse your a-- off. Practice. Then practice more.

> "The dictionary is the only place that success comes before work."
> —Vince Lombardi
>
> "Champions keep playing unit they get it right."
> —Billie Jean King

Be a Good Listener

Especially in new situations; it is ok not to have the answers.
You can lead while learning and leveraging the strength of others.
Allow others to contribute—everybody wins this way.
Find the value in alternative perspectives!
Thank people for their input and mean it.
Get over yourself . . . you don't always have to be right to be in control.
(Note: there is a thin line between confident and arrogant—be confidant and humble.)

> *"Be a good listener. Your ears will never get you into trouble."*
> —Frank Tyger

Be Flexible!

Say "yes" to opportunities that were not in your plans.
Make the most and learn from every opportunity.
Especially say yes to the opportunities that scare you.

"If you're offered a seat on a rocket ship don't ask what seat, just get on."
—Sheryl Sandberg

● ● ●

"Life is about using the whole box of crayons."
—RuPaul

● ● ●

"Arrange whatever pieces come your way."
—Virginia Woolf

● ● ●

"Blessed are the flexible, for they shall never be bent out of shape."
—Michael McGriffy, MD

● ● ●

"Happiness often sneaks in through a door you didn't know you left open."
—John Barrymore

● ● ●

"Not knowing when the dawn will come, I open every door."
—Emily Dickinson

● ● ●

"Remember that not getting what you want is sometimes a wonderful stroke of luck."
—Dalai Lama

Persuasive Presentation Skills Are a Prerequisite for Success

Remember the three P's—and they are not panic, puke, and pass out.
They are for: prepare, practice and passionate!
Persuading people with your voice is power!
Speak up—have a unique voice.

Be Boldly Expressive

Don't ever lose that rebel yell.

> "Freedom lies in being bold."
>
> —Robert Frost

Speaking with Confidence

Being able to present well and persuade people with your message is very powerful. I used to feel faint just thinking about raising my hand and speaking. You cannot be a leader if you cannot speak with confidence. One of my favorite bosses, Chris, gave me the best advice and no, it is not the old "see-them-in-their-underwear" trick. He said just tell your story as you would to a friend, no matter how many people there are in the room. Be enthusiastic, personable, and confident, as it is your story. Nobody else knows it. If you mess up, don't apologize, or even pause. Just keep going with a smile as nobody else will even notice. Everyone there wants to hear your story *and* they want you to tell it well. People want you to win so speak with confidence.

Practice Positive Self-Talk

What you say to yourself is more important than what anyone else says.
Rewire any negativity and support yourself no matter what.
Develop a self-motivating mantra and tell it to yourself often.

> "To move the world, we must first move ourselves."   —Socrates
>
> "The way you treat yourself sets the standards for others."
>
> —Sonya Friedman

> "We become what we think about most of the time and that's the strangest secret."
> —Earl Nightingale

> "Change your thoughts and change your world."
> —Norman Vincent Peale

Preparing/Rituals Before a Big Day

Research, practice, run it by people you trust and *rehearse* your a-- off.
Use positive self-talk to cheer yourself on.
Imagine your "hero" talking you through it; what would they recommend?
Take positive visualization all the way—see it going perfectly in your head.
Imagine a cheering crowd of fans; everyone is rooting for you!
Believe in yourself! Go for it!

> "All it takes is faith and trust."
> —Peter Pan, from the movie *Peter Pan*

> "A man is but a product of his thoughts. What he thinks he becomes."
> —Gandhi

Be a Rock Star

This is a real over share alert. But this "exercise" works for me and I have been doing it for years. It is natural and actually a benefit to get a bit nervous before a presentation or major career event. It amps you up, ensures you are at your best, and it can fuel your power. We have all heard the secret of imagining it all going well—the power of positive thinking. I am likely to take this winning principal to unusual heights. I imagine I am Madonna (in leather and ridiculously high boots) walking onto a stage in front of screaming fans. Younger readers may want to select Rihanna or Beyoncé. It is awesome and quite a rush to see and hear those adoring fans. What will your pre-game positive fantasy ritual be next time? If it is embarrassing go ahead and keep it quiet for now. But definitely stretch with this exercise. You might also want to try this trick—go into the restroom right before your meeting and strike a major victory pose and say, "I got this!" This will pump up your adrenaline and allow you to enter the room feeling like a winner.

Be Present

"Enjoy the little things for someday you may look back and realize they were the big things."
—Robert Brault

"Think big thoughts but relish small pleasures."
—H. Jackson Brown, Jr.

"Normal day, let me be aware of the blessing you are."
—Mary Jane Irion

"Look at everything as though you are seeing it either for the first time or the last time."
—Betty Smith

Practice Strategic Disengagement

Resting is important; ensure you get enough.
Having hobbies and enjoying them is critical.
Vacations are lifesavers; and are not optional.
When overwhelmed, step away from your desk.
Take a walk, meditate, or at least give your brain a break.
Restore balance by finding a work friend and bounce some ideas around.
Make the most of every day and every moment.

"Doing nothing is better than being busy doing nothing."
—Lao Tzu

"It is important from time to time to slow down, to go away by yourself, and simply be."
—Eileen Caddy

Be Observant

Find fascination in everything.
Look for inspiration in unusual places.
Find beauty all around you.
Answers are usually already present.
Share your discoveries with others.

> *"What we see depends mostly on what we look for."*
> —John Lubbock
>
> • • •
>
> *"There are always flowers for those who want to see them."*
> —Henri Matisse
>
> • • •
>
> *"The world is full of magic things, patiently waiting for our senses to grow sharper."*
> —W. B. Yeats

Be Generous. Share the Credit

Everyone loves a giver—be generous; share the spotlight.
However, take the credit too.
Say,"*'The team and I'* are proud of this success."

> *"Whatever we possess becomes of double value when we have the opportunity of sharing it with others."* —Jean Nicolas Bouilly

Be of Service

Volunteer your time to help others.
Make someone else's day . . . even if just with a kind comment.
Be sure your work has purpose.
Share what you have learned with others.

> *"You give little when you give of your possessions. It is when you give of yourself that you truly give."* —Kahlil Gibran
>
> • • •
>
> *"Aim above morality. Be not simply good, be good for something."* —Henry David Thoreau
>
> • • •
>
> *"A hero is any person really intent on making this a better place for all people."* —Maya Angelou

Be Humble

You can be confident and maintain your humility.
Keep your feet on the ground no matter how high up you go.
Nobody likes a bragger; everyone loves a humble hero.

> "Our ego is our silent partner—too often with a controlling interest."
> —Cullen Hightower

Just a Boy from Philly

Dennis gave me my first job at Disney. I say "gave" as I am sure he had other more qualified candidates. He was the vice president of sales for Disney's Home Video division. His office was huge yet his ego non-existent. A milkman's son, he loved the story of how hard his father worked and how he started at the bottom and worked his way up from a sales representative to head of sales. We likely bonded over our humble roots and big dreams. I won't forget his many style lessons. Gratitude and pride radiated from his smile. He was humble, yet possessed a clearly confident presence. He loved his family, his job, his work team, and his baseball team—I am not sure he ever articulated it with words but you could just tell. Dennis is now a president at Paramount. I am sure still rooting for his beloved baseball team and we all still root for him.

> "Believe in yourself. Have faith in your abilities. Without a humble but reasonable confidence in your own powers you cannot be successful or happy."
> —Norman Vincent Peale

> "Be thankful for what you do have; you will end up having more. If you concentrate on what you don't have, you will never have enough."
> —Oprah Winfrey

> "Happiness cannot be traveled to, owned, earned, or consumed. Happiness is the spiritual experience of living every moment with love, grace, and gratitude."
> —Denis Waitley

> "We can only be said to be alive in those moments when our hearts are conscious of our treasures."
> —Thornton Wilder

Take Accountability. Everything Matters

Stuff will go wrong, especially if you are going to be a risk-taker.
Accept responsibility. Even if someone else messed up on your project or idea.
State the issue and quickly make suggestions of what can be learned.
Recap and share—promote the valuable lesson and the future plan.
Be timely, learn, share, and move on quickly.

> "To admit that you were wrong is to declare that you are wiser than you were before."
>
> —Unknown

Be Persistent

> "Ambition is the path to success. Persistence is the vehicle you arrive in."
>
> —Bill Bradley

• • •

> "I don't need easy, I just need possible."
>
> —Bethany Hamilton, from the movie *Soul Surfer*

• • •

> "When the world says 'give up,' hope whispers 'try it one more time.'"
>
> —Unknown

• • •

> "Your most valuable asset can be your willingness to persist longer than anyone else."
>
> —Brian Tracy

Be Honest

> "Being honest may not get you a lot of friends, but it'll get you the right ones."
>
> —John Lennon

Be Daring

> "Whatever there be of progress in life comes not through adaptation but through daring."
>
> —Henry Miller

> *"Fortune sides with him who dares."* —Virgil
>
> *"Inhale confidence, exhale doubt"* —Unknown

Be Unordinary

Have a bold act.
Wear what you want.
It's your show.

> *"Either write something worth reading or do something worth writing."* —Benjamin Franklin
>
> *"If you are not willing to risk the unusual, you will have to settle for ordinary."* —Jim Rohn
>
> *"The only people who never tumble are those who never mount the high wire. This is your moment. Own it."* —Oprah Winfrey
>
> *"Blessed are the weird people—the poets, misfits, mystics, painters, and troubadours, for they teach us to see the world through different eyes."* —Jacob Norby

Wear What You Want

Don't confuse "presence" and "style" with wardrobe choices. I think the dress for success rules are the biggest crap. You need to be you. Steve Jobs wore black jeans and a black turtleneck *every day*. John Lasseter wears a Hawaiian shirt and I swear the same old brown loafers *every day*. I should not dole out advice here as I wore a short skirt and big silly hat to an interview for a job I really wanted. Shockingly I did get that job. I still like to rebel on these how-to-dress rules and take risks. I still wear a J. Crew tee shirt if I have to wear a suit somewhere. And open toe shoes even in December. I am also very fond of clothes which feature animals. Wear what makes you feel unique, confident, and comfortable. Don't be afraid to be original and stretch some of the rules to be true to you. Wear the suit and that pressed shirt if you must. Just be sure you are rebelling somewhere else to be true to the real you inside. Fighting against what we deem "crap" keeps us real.

> *"Your need for acceptance can make you invisible in this world. Risk being seen in all of your glory."*
> —Jim Carrey

Trouble Happens. Remain Calm

> *"Expect trouble as an inevitable part of life and repeat to yourself the most comforting words of all; this too shall pass."*
> —Ann Landers

> *"Eventually all things fall into place. Until then, laugh at the confusion, live for the moment, and know everything happens for a reason."*
> —Albert Schweitzer

Work Smarter, Not Longer

It would be rare to have a supervisor who stood over you and told you to work seventy-five hours a week, forget about exercise, seeing your family. You would also have guilt if you leave without completing all your work. Recognize as soon as possible that all those messages are fully self-induced and you are likely making yourself feel guilty unnecessarily. Once you accept this, you can embrace the fact that you are in control. Only you can set your priorities as only you know what makes you happy. You will always be your most important boss.

> *"Tension is who you think you should be. Relaxation is who you are."*
> —Chinese Proverb

> *"Work hard. Play hard. Rest easy."*
> —Eva Steortz

Keep Perspective

> *"Remember that stress doesn't come from what's going on in your life. It comes from your thoughts about what's going on in your life."*
> —Andrew Bernstein

> "Give your stress wings and let it fly away." —Terri Guillemets
>
> "The greatest weapon against stress is our ability to choose one thought over another." —William James

Love and Kindness

Bring your heart to work with you.
Treat people with kindness.
Ensure your work and theirs has meaning.

> "The highest form of wisdom is kindness." —Talmud
>
> "Remember that everyone you meet is afraid of something, loves something, and has lost something." —H. Jackson Brown, Jr.
>
> "Tenderness and kindness are not signs of weakness and despair, but manifestations of strength and resolution." —Kahlil Gibran
>
> "There are three ways to ultimate success: The first is to be kind. The second is to be kind. The third is to be kind." —Mr. Rogers

Lead with Your Heart

We are all just kids at heart who want to love and be loved. Another favorite boss of mine was famous for keeping it real. He laughed freely and took his shoes off in meetings. When I worked for him in the toy division, he would often stop his staff meetings and tell stories. Once around the holidays, he stopped in the middle of a rather intense business review where the head of finance was literally pounding his fist on the table over some unfavorable sales numbers, and Tim very emotionally said, "Let's hold on a minute. We should all be proud of what we do, and remember why we do it. Let's just take a minute to imagine the joy on children's faces on Christmas morning as they open up their princess dolls and *Cars* race sets. The work we do matters way more than the numbers." Not a dry eye around the conference table. Talk about bringing everything into perspective and leading from the heart. I would follow Tim anywhere. We all would. Tim continues his impressive career climb at Activision after many years climbing the ranks at Disney and Mattel. I love it when the good guys win.

"The most important thing in life is to learn how to give out love, and to let it come in." —Morrie Schwartz

"The best and most beautiful things in the world cannot be seen or even touched, they must be felt with the heart." —Helen Keller

"If you could only love enough, you could be the most powerful person in the world." —Emmet Fox

"Success is not so much what you have as it is what you are." —Jim Rohn

"There is only one happiness in this life. To love and be loved." —George Sand

Be Grateful

Be grateful for what you do have. Make the most of those gifts.
Be grateful for your challenges as they make you stronger.
Every day is a new day to begin again and be even more positive and
 productive.
Keep moving forward with confidence and gratitude.

"Don't limit your challenges. Challenge your limits." —Jerry Dunn

● ● ●

"Gratitude is the single most important ingredient to living a successful and fulfilled life." —Jack Canfield

● ● ●

"Gratitude and attitude are not challenges, they are choices." —Robert Braathe

● ● ●

"Gratitude makes sense of our past, brings peace for today, and creates a vision for tomorrow." —Melody Beattie

● ● ●

"When I hear someone say, 'life is hard' I am always tempted to ask 'compared to what?'" —Sydney Harris

Possessing Positive Style

Recrafting Your Style Story

Perhaps now you will want to revisit the three words you selected to define yourself. These words can become your guiding force as you go forth in life. A simple way to motivate yourself every day.

Just like in planning for a presentation, creating a brand new positioning statement or even an important discussion with a friend, you need to prepare and practice how you are going to tell your style story.

When someone asks what you do, you now won't have to respond with your job title or flounder for the words. Build a story around your style. Use colorful words which are personal to you. Don't use common jargon like the words filling up your resume. No "results oriented," strategic," "detail oriented," "team player." Get creative and give yourself the special story you deserve.

Position yourself for success and for inner peace knowing that you are in control and are ready for all that comes next. What do I do? "I am a saucy southern sage on a mission to be fully fearless while inspiring and supporting others to aim high in their careers."

Chapter 6

Self-Motivation Matters Most: Your Career Path Is Up to You

Work Hard and You Will Succeed—Yeah, No, Not Really!

Work smart. Provide vision, new ideas, innovation, and solutions.
Seventy hours a week has no rewards—*Trust me here.*
A new idea, process, product idea, service, etc.—that is what will propel you.
Ensure you are enjoying your work or do something different.

Have a Five-Year Plan—Use It as a Guideline, Not a Rule

It is important to set goals, timelines, and plan your path.
However, flexibility is key; sometimes an opportunity to learn is in disguise.
Evaluate and take advantage of unexpected experiences in your path.
Be open—sometimes a gift is right in front of you, yet not on your to do list.

> *"We must be willing to let go of the life we've planned so as to have the life that is waiting for us."* —Joseph Campbell
>
> *"It is good to have an end to journey toward, but it is the journey that matters in the end."* —Ursula K. Le Guin

Move Closer to Your Ultimate Goal

Take small steps toward your dream.
Just keep getting closer any way you can.
Volunteer if you have to. This will get you more experience.

Be Bold!

> *"Whatever you can do, or dream, you can begin it. Boldness has genius, power, and magic in it."* —Goethe

Aim High!

"You have to have a dream for your dream to come true."
—Denis Waitley

"If we did all of the things we are capable of, we would astound ourselves."
—Thomas Edison

"Shoot for the moon. Even if you miss, you will land among the stars."
—Norman Vincent Peale

Have a Sense of Urgency

Don't just wish, take action.
Don't just hope, develop a plan.

"The start is what stops most people."
—Don Shula

"The secret of getting ahead is getting started."
—Mark Twain

"If everything seems under control, you're just not going fast enough."
—Mario Andretti

"Go for it now. The future is promised to no one."
—Wayne W. Dyer

"There are seven days in the week and some day is not one of them."
—Unknown

"If you spend too much time thinking about a thing, you'll never get it done."
Bruce Lee

Take Time to Think

Scenario planning, pro and con analysis, or just let your mind wander. Thinking is important work.

"Don't judge each day by the harvest you reap but by the seeds that you plant."
—Ralph Waldo Emerson

Make Good Choices

Everyday your choices impact your dreams.
Everything you do is up to you.
Every choice should align with who you have decided to be.
Every choice matters. Choose wisely.

> *"It is choice not chance that determines your destiny."* —Jean Nidetch
>
> *"The bad news is time flies, the good news is you're the pilot."*
> —Michael Altshuler

Fish Where the Fish Are

Andy, Disney Consumer Product's second chairman during my tenure, was an accountant by trade so everything was black and white to him. He had a brilliant ability to look at an opportunity or challenge with absolute clarity and simplicity. One of his first steps as a leader in a steeply declining business was to set crystal clear priorities. His direction was to focus on the top five retail accounts and the top five Disney characters. Such a simple idea. Fish where the fish are. It was focus by force. Focus all efforts here or suffer the consequences of going off course. Nobody wanted to deal with disagreeing with Andy. It was hard to rationalize not following this direction, or any of his plans based on its higher return on investment and simple strategic logic. While he brought a lot of incredible strategies to our team, it was this first one with its memorable story telling headline, "fish where the fish are," that was a primary contributor to twelve years of incredible growth. The lesson is simple. Prioritize. Focus. Make wise choices and win.

Be a Planner and a Doer

Wishing on a star is good.
Developing an action plan is better.
Going for it no matter what is best!

> *"A goal without a plan is just a wish."* —Antoine de Saint-Exupéry
>
> *"The most difficult thing is to act. The rest is just tenacity."*
> —Amelia Earhart
>
> *"Make each day your masterpiece."* —John Wooden

> *"Make no small plans for they have no power to stir the soul."*
> —Niccolo Machiavelli

> *"Dreaming after all is a form of planning."* —Gloria Steinem

> *"Reach high for stars are hidden in your soul. Dream deep, for every dream precedes a goal."* —Pamela Vaull Starr

Stay Passionate About Your Personal Goals

Never give up.
Pursue your passions.
Especially the wild stretch "what if" goals.

> *"It's always too early to quit."* —Norman Vincent Peale

> *"Success isn't permanent and failure isn't fatal; it's the courage to continue that counts."* —Mike Ditka

> *"It's hard to beat a person who never gives up."* —Babe Ruth

Stretch and Do It!

"It always seems impossible until it's done." —Nelson Mandela

● ● ●

"One finds limits by pushing them." —Herbert Simon

● ● ●

"If you are going to doubt something, doubt your limits." —Don Ward

Be Fearless

Ask to attend meetings. Ask for and offer input.
Send articles or ideas to executives of all levels.
Call and ask leaders in your field for input and support.
Invite leaders to coffee suggesting interest in their career advice.
Apply for jobs a bit higher than your credentials—*stretch.*

"Reach for the sky."   —Woody, from the movie *Toy Story*

• • •

"Playing it safe is the riskiest choice we can ever make."
—Sarah Ban Breathnach

• • •

"Follow your hopes and not your fears."   —Jody Bower

• • •

"Don't worry about failures, worry about the chances you miss when you don't even try."   —Jack Canfield

• • •

"To live a creative life, we must lose our fear of being wrong."
—Joseph Chilton Pearce

• • •

"Too many of us are not living our dreams because we are living our fears."   —Les Brown

• • •

"Our deepest fear is not that we are inadequate. Our deepest fear is that we are powerful beyond measure. It is our Light, not our Darkness, that most frightens us."   —Marianne Williamson

• • •

"I've had a lot of worries in my life, most of which never happened."   —Mark Twain

• • •

"Courage is resistance to fear, mastery of fear, not absence of fear."   —Mark Twain

A Good Idea Should Scare You

"An idea that is not dangerous is unworthy to be called an idea at all."
— Elbert Hubbard

● ● ●

"Life shrinks or expands in proportion to one's courage."
— Anais Nin

● ● ●

"Everything you have ever wanted is on the other side of fear."
— George Addair

● ● ●

"All growth is a leap in the dark, a spontaneous unpremeditated act without benefit of experience."
— Henry Miller

Crazy Often Works

I got my job at Young & Rubicam's entertainment marketing agency by doing something kind of crazy. I would have never done it in my thirties or forties but at twenty-five, what is there to lose? I sent a fax (email had not yet been invented, can you imagine?) for seven days in a row with a simple and straightforward "Why You Should Hire Eva" message. I remember thinking at the time, this is either going to be awesome or they will call the authorities and have me arrested for stalking. I got the interview. I was so excited. Then I wore a short frilly skirt and a silly black hat with red rose buds. I got the job despite my wild wardrobe choice. I have missed the "take-crazy-chances and go-for-it" Eva. She is back in her fifties and finally almost fully fearless. I am a bit beyond the short skirt, but I do believe the right hat could still be quite impactful.

"If at first the idea is not absurd, then there is no hope for it."
— Albert Einstein

● ● ●

"You must have chaos within you to give birth to a dancing star."
— Friedrich Nietzsche

● ● ●

"You were once wild. Don't let them tame you." — Isadora Duncan

Trust Yourself

"It is not the mountain that we conquer but ourselves."
—Sir Edmund Hillary

"Once we believe in ourselves, we risk curiosity, wonder, spontaneous delight or any experience that reveals the human spirit."
—E. E. Cummings

Be Brave

"Success is not final, failure is not fatal; it is the courage to continue that counts."
—Winston Churchill

• • •

"If you had a chance to change your fate, would you?"
—Merida, from the movie *Brave*

• • •

"Courage is being scared to death and saddling up anyway."
—John Wayne

• • •

"The key to success is to focus your conscious mind on things you desire not things you fear."
—Brian Tracy

• • •

"We all have the ability. We just don't all have the courage to follow our dreams and to follow the signs."
—Paulo Coelho

• • •

"The task we must set for ourselves is not to feel secure, but to be able to tolerate insecurity."
—Erich Fromm

Trust Your Instincts

"Do not follow the ideas of others. Learn to listen to the voice inside yourself."
—Dogen

"There is no certainty. There is only adventure."
—Roberto Assagioli

Don't Lose Your Curiosity

Ask a lot of questions and listen.
What motivates people?
How does it work and what would make it better?
Where are the new opportunities? When can we try something new?
Understand how your role fits in with the big picture.

> *"Curiosity will conquer fear even more than bravery will."*
>
> —James Stephens
>
> *"When you're curious, you find lots of interesting things to do. And one thing it takes to accomplish something is courage."*
>
> —Walt Disney

Create Your Own Path

Ask what success looks like for you and follow your heart there.
Don't set unrealistic timetables for your journey.
Enjoy the adventure and the side streets along the way

> *"It does not matter how slowly you go so long as you do not stop."*
>
> —Confucius

Be Proactive

Don't wait.
Don't whine.
Don't let opportunities pass you by.

> *"If your ship doesn't come in, swim out to it."* —Jonathan Winters

Take Time to Celebrate Your Achievements. Take Time for Tea. Or Better, Champagne!

Celebrate success.
Celebrate progress not perfection.
Celebrate each other and the collaboration.

> *"Celebrate the happiness that friends are always giving. Make every day a holiday to celebrate just living."*
>
> —Amanda Bradley
>
> *"Happiness is not a state to arrive at, but a manner of traveling."*
>
> —Margaret Lee Runbeck

Carnivals, Music, and Massages

Don't feel guilty about having fun at work. My best leaders just planned it into our curriculum calling it "strategic disengagement." They participated so we all did. We had employee talent contests, carnivals in the parking lot, appreciation massages in the conference room, and sometimes just a kitchen full of bagels. You will be doing your boss a favor if you recommend fun employee events. It is guaranteed that team output will increase in quality and quantity if you reward people with *fun* for work well done. Thank you, Andy, for pulling out your guitar and hosting concerts on the lawn for us. And mostly for prioritizing people. In the end, you agreed that your most impressive achievements were because you mobilized the power of your *people*. We sure had fun winning.

> *"You can dream, create, design and build the most wonderful place in the world, but it takes people to make the dream a reality."*
>
> —Walt Disney

Champagne Toasts and Celebrating Success

The home entertainment business was on fire in the early nineties but of course *The Lion King* set a new high bar. The leader of the video group at the time was known for being pretty tough but she pulled off one of the best celebrations of success moves I have ever seen. During a typical town hall meeting, both doors burst open and waiters carrying trays of champagne entered and handed one to everyone. A massive team toast. Celebrating success is critical. Make it memorable. I will never forget that day, Ann. Cheers!

Take Risks

Lead, but don't go alone. Get mentors and leaders who support and guide you.

Ensure your plan is supported and backed up with solid fact-based rationale.

Do your homework, be strategic, build a plan, and then *go for it.*

Change only comes from being courageous enough to try something new.

> *"Let's make some magic!"* —Genie from the movie, *Aladdin*
>
> *"Courage is being scared to death and saddling up any way"*
> —John Wayne
>
> *"A smooth sea never made a skillful sailor."* —English proverb

Ask for Feedback, Listen, *and* Learn

Don't bother asking if you won't admit you could do with some improving.

Learn to love feedback—especially hard-core constructive feedback.

Feedback is a gift—even when it hurts.

Be honest with yourself—how do you think you are progressing?

Secret to knowing if you are succeeding—are people cheering you on?

If you don't hear cheering . . . then you need to work on your relationships.

Listen, Edit, Learn, and Move Ahead

> *"Let nothing dim the light that shines from within."*
> —Maya Angelou

Find Your Strengths

> *"The very things that held you down are going to carry you up, and up, and up!"*
> —Timothy Mouse, from the movie *Dumbo*

Ask for Tough Love

I had been a director of Promotions for seven years and was getting very impatient and eager to get to the next level. My boss at the time, Jessi, was sarcastic, feisty, and fun. I liked her a lot. I asked her to give me feedback and coach me on how I could get promoted. Oh my goodness, I didn't realize the intensity of the training that was to follow. Right after a meeting she would pull me aside and replay how I handled situations too "assertively." She would explain candidly how I could have listened and been more positive, and how I could have improved my argument with facts and more professional presence. She also gave me heads up on higher-level executives I needed to win over and how to do it. She unleashed loads of tough love on me that was very hard to hear about my style and how others perceived me. It was pretty much daily kicks to the gut for a year. Once I had made real tangible and noticeable style changes, she promoted me to VP. It's a rare gift to find someone who will tell you things you need to hear. Find someone who will give you this tough love. Do it now! You will be grateful to them forever. And you should return the favor to someone you work with someday soon.

"You may not realize it when it happens, but a kick in the teeth may be the best thing in the world for you."
—Walt Disney

"Life has a way of testing a person's will, either by having nothing happen at all or by having everything happen at once."
—Paulo Coelho

Keep Moving Forward

Ahead is always the right course.
Positive action is always the right choice.

"When life gets you down . . . just keep swimming."
—Dory, from the movie *Finding Nemo*

"If you are going through hell, keep going."
—Winston Churchill

"We cannot start over, but we can begin now and make a new ending."
—Zig Ziglar

• • •

"Man maintains his balance, poise and sense of security only as he is moving forward."
—Maxwell Maltz

• • •

"The past cannot be changed. The future is still in your power."
—Mary Pickford

• • •

"The only time you should look back is to see how far you have come."
—Kevin Hart

• • •

"Nothing behind me, everything ahead of me as is so ever on the road."
—Jack Kerouac

• • •

"Action is the foundational key to all success."
—Pablo Picasso

• • •

"I will go anywhere, as long as it is forward."
—David Livingston

• • •

"You only have your thoughts and dreams ahead of you. You are someone. You mean something."
—Batman

Do Your To-Do's

"The greatest weariness comes from work not done."
—Eric Hoffer

"Dreams don't work unless you do."
—John Maxwell

Trust Your Instincts

After I had been VP for a few years and I thought everything was going great, I was asked to report to one of my previous peers. What? Yet another kick to the teeth. What was I missing? I was popular, I received great reviews but once again I was not moving up. So, I asked for a career coach to demonstrate I was serious about progressing. I seriously did not realize how badly I needed another round of training. Turns out my greatest strengths were becoming blind spots. My positivity was being perceived as cheerleading versus serious business strategy and once I was honest with myself I realized it was indeed true. I wasn't taking the time to build strong rational for my recommended new ideas. I had gotten too comfortable with my position and was just pushing positivity without really being persuasive. I made immediate changes and started saying the words "fact based rationale" and "strategy" a lot. Soon thereafter I had the opportunity to work on a big project with our chairman and CFO. And soon after that, I got a much larger role and team. Throughout your whole career, you must maintain your self-awareness and do not get comfortable. You have to admit when you need to make changes. You can sense these things if you are honest with yourself. Thank you to my career coach Lisa for helping me identify and rectify my blind spots. Thank you for coaching me and giving me that much appreciated and needed lifetime guarantee.

"I will love the light for it shows me the way, yet I will endure the darkness because it shows me the stars."

—Og Mandino

You Can Do Anything You Set Your Mind To

Mostly true! Be ambitious but realistic and *honest* about your true goals!
Focus on leveraging your strengths.
Acknowledge that your strengths in excess can be a weakness.
Be resourceful in covering your weaknesses; delegate or ask for help.
Be truthful about what you really want out of life and don't forget *love* and family.
Ensure you are setting your goals higher than your comfort zone.
Believe you can, and you will.

"What lies behind us and what lies before us are tiny matters compared to what lies within us." —Ralph Waldo Emerson

● ● ●

"To get something you've never had, you have to do something you've never done." —Thomas Jefferson

● ● ●

"Who is the happier man, he who has braved the storm of life and lived or he who has stayed securely on the shore and merely existed?" —Hunter S. Thompson

Believe!

"To accomplish great things, we must not only act, but also dream; not only plan, but also believe." —Anatole France

● ● ●

"Take the first step in faith. You don't have to see the whole staircase, just the first step." —Martin Luther King, Jr.

● ● ●

"Choose to be optimistic. It feels better." —Dalai Lama

Imagine the Possibilities

"Imagination is everything. It's the preview of life's coming attractions." —Albert Einstein

You Don't Have to Grow Up

Your childhood imagination is one of your greatest gifts.
Pretending is one of the secrets.
Believing anything is possible is a rare asset.

"Life's like a movie, write your own ending. Keep believing, keep pretending." —Jim Henson

Aim Even Higher!

> *"Don't let what you can't do, stop you from what you can do."*
> —John Wooden

Prioritize the "What Ifs"

> *"Fantasy and reality often overlap."*
> —Walt Disney
>
> *"You can fly."*
> —Peter Pan, from the movie *Peter Pan*

Dream Big

> *"Never give up on what you really want to do. The person with the big dreams is more powerful than the one with all the facts."*
> —Albert Einstein

Go for It!

> *"You miss 100% of the shots you don't take."*   —Wayne Gretzky

Be Unstoppable

Obstacles, beware.
Doubters, step aside.

> *"It's not what you achieve, it's what you overcome. That's what defines your career."*
> —Carlton Fisk
>
> *"Never ever ever ever give up."*
> —Winston Churchill
>
> *"The difference between try and triumph is just a little umph."*
> —Marvin Phillips

Self-Motivation Matters Most

Be Determined

> "This one step: choosing a goal and sticking to it changes everything."
> —Scott Reed

> "A vision keeps the wealthy soul focused on the path and not the boulders."
> —Michael Norwood

Be Stronger Than Your Excuses

> "Courage doesn't always roar. Sometimes it is the quiet voice at the end of the day saying, 'I will try again tomorrow.'"
> —Mary Ann Radmacher

> "Real obstacles can be overcome; it is only the imaginary ones that are unconquerable."
> —Theodore N. Vail

> "I am the one constant obstacle to my own momentum."
> —Pete Vellucci, Jr.

Play to Win

> "Winning isn't everything, but wanting to win is." —Vince Lombardi

The Unwavering Always Win

> "The greatest pleasure in life is doing what people say you cannot do."
> —Walter Bagehot

> "Our greatest glory is not in never failing, but in rising every time we fall."
> —Confucius

Find Your Purpose

Take time to understand what drives you.
Honestly assess what motivates you.
Articulate with passion your goals and why.
Be clear with yourself and others what your intentions are.
Make sure you are using your gifts for the greatest good.

"In a gentle way, you can shake the world." —Gandhi

"Effort and courage are not enough without purpose and direction." —John F. Kennedy

"You are here to enable the divine purpose of the universe to unfold. That is how important you are." —Eckhart Tolle

Puppies, Monkeys, and Balloons...Oh My!

In promoting new films to retail buyers, it was customary to take several scenes from the movies out to company's headquarters to tell the story and promote the tie-in toy and apparel business opportunities. Of course, it was exciting to see new films months before they come out in theaters. When I was planning these events, it became like planning a party and often was like a trip to the zoo. For *101 Dalmatians*, I unleashed a dozen puppies into the crowd. For *Tarzan*, I hired a trainer with a bird and a monkey. The Events Team loved and hated me. The balloons and confetti canons seemed lame and tame compared to my insistence on wildlife. They were called "road shows" and I took the "show" part to new levels. If you are going to do a show, then by all means put on a memorable one! Plan some surprises and prioritize what would be most unexpected. And remember, everyone loves animals.

Promote Your Successes like a Rock Band

Make your mark; name your projects something sexy and promote them.
Celebrate and document successes: emails, billboards, press, and parties.
Don't feel bad tooting your own horn, your future is up to *you!*
Do share the credit, and document the benefits for the company.

Focus

As you choose your goals for next year, prioritize.
Pick one that has been on your mind and in your heart.
Focus on one major game changer for you *and* for your team.

Game Changers

Prioritize each day's must do list—pick the top three.
Do one thing a day that scares the s--- out of you!
What could be a game changer? Do that *first* as it is most important.
Go for what seems impossible.

Go Big or Go Home!

> *"You're entirely, bonkers. But I'll tell you a secret. All the best people are."* —Alice, from *Alice in Wonderland*
>
> *"It always seems impossible until it is done."* —Nelson Mandela
>
> *"Do one thing every day that scares you."* —Eleanor Roosevelt

Coloring Mickey Outside the Lines

When a new chairman was named from Nike, there was a massive organizational overhaul with layoffs and new hires happening at rapid speed. This is what you need to know; when organizational leadership changes happen, there will be some chaos. Sometimes things will seem crazy. A whole team of new non-Disney, non-entertainment executives came into the company ready to make their mark. Talk about challenging the status quo. Many of their ideas were deemed sacrilegious by Disney corporate and us Disney longtimers. Their idea of humor was pairing an image of Peter Pan and the editorial line "I hang out with fairies." While all finally agreed that this was taking creative liberties a tad too far for a family brand, in general the notion of adding irreverent humor, and not being so precious with traditional character art led to a very fresh approach and enormous business growth. Roger, your time at Disney was short, but your radical impact had serious longevity. Thanks for rocking the boat, testing the boundaries, shocking us, and being a major game changer. I miss the way you would look over your reading glasses, anticipating our stunned faces during your presentations.

Take **Risks.** Make **Mistakes.** Learn **Lessons.**

"You have a right to experiment with your life. You will make mistakes. And they are right too." —Anais Nin

"Dream big and dare to fail." —Norman D. Vaughan

"Mistakes are the dues one pays for a full life." —Sophia Loren

"Anyone who has never made a mistake has never tried anything new." —Albert Einstein

"You make mistakes. Mistakes don't make you."

—Maxwell Maltz

Let It Be **Easy**

Opportunities and choices are always present.
Be open. And follow your heart.
Expect the best.
Trust your path.

"If you live the questions, life will move you to the answers."
—Deepak Chopra

Give Yourself a **Break**

We are all our own worst critics—remember that and be kind to yourself.
Don't give yourself a herculean to-do list and then beat yourself up
   when it's not all done.
90% is an A. Especially when speed-to-market and high-volume output
   is expected.
Never give up. You could be just on the verge of your greatest
   accomplishment.

"My, my what beautiful blossoms we have this year. But look, this one's late. But I'll bet that when it blooms it will be the most beautiful of all." —Fa Zhou, from the movie *Mulan*

> *"The task we must set for ourselves is not to feel secure, but to be able to tolerate insecurity."*
>
> —Erich Fromm

Cheer for Yourself

Be your own best friend, publicist, and advocate.
Manage your self-talk—be your own career advisor AND cheerleader.
If you think something negative; balance with a positive affirmation.
(Example: Eva, you suck at data analysis, yet you excel at big idea creation.)

> *"Embrace the glorious mess that you are."* —Elizabeth Gilbert

Compete with Yourself. Play to Win

Competition is important; you want to be the best at what you do.
Strive to be the best you; not just better than the others.
You will aim higher by being the best you!
Exceed your own expectations.

> *"It is better to conquer yourself than to win a thousand battles. Then the victory is yours. It cannot be taken away."* —Buddha

> *"If you're still looking for that one person who can change your life, take a look in the mirror."* —Ritu Ghatourey
>
> *"There are no traffic jams along the extra mile."* —Roger Staubach
>
> *"Mastering others is strength. Mastering yourself is true power."* —Lao Tzu
>
> *"As we let our own light shine, we unconsciously give other people permission to do the same."* —Nelson Mandela

There Is Something About Mary

It can be hard to support a peer ten years younger who proclaims her intentions to run the entire company upon her arrival onto the team. Someone who raises the bar so high, the rest of us just go to an actual bar to commiserate. Mary was not immediately popular and that did not appear to be her priority. She was there to win. However, she quickly became aware of the risks of blind ambition. She was a very hard and smart worker and every time she was promoted she insisted on doing the work herself before she delegated it to others. She quickly realized she needed to be aware of and rally with the team around her. While brilliant at managing up, she also learned the importance of prioritizing the team below her and her peers. She really did earn her fast career progression. She coupled her big ideas with strong leadership.

Don't be afraid to give support to these wildly motivated, driven, overly ambitious people you meet along the way. Be inspired by their commitment to excel. And realize you likely have some life lessons to share with them, too. Don't let your jealousy or fear keep you from an amazing friendship. These young trailblazers are likely to play a critical role in your career adventure.

> *"One way to get the most out of life is to look upon it as an adventure."*
> —William Feather

Seek Adventure

Embrace every opportunity.
Do something new every day.
Stretch. Enjoy being outside of your comfort zone.

> *"The only question in life is whether or not you are going to answer a hearty 'yes!' to your adventure."* —Joseph Campbell
>
> *"I don't want to end up simply having visited this world."*
> —Mary Oliver

Push Yourself—Even When You Are Doing Great

When you are on top, take a class, get a coach, or ask for hard-core feedback!
Challenge yourself to always stay ahead of your own expectations.

> "The time to repair the roof is when the sun is shining."
> —John F. Kennedy
>
> "You are always a student, never a master. You have to keep moving forward."
> —Conrad Hall

Don't Get Too Comfortable!

> "Even if you are on the right track, you'll get run over if you just sit there."
> —Will Rogers
>
> "Only those who will risk going too far can possibly find out how far one can go."
> —T. S. Eliot

Imagine the Possibilities

> "Limitations live only in our minds. But if we use our imaginations, our possibilities become limitless." —Jamie Paolinetti

Don't Accept Your Own Excuses

Give yourself tough love; don't accept your own excuses.
Treat your own growth as you would any project for which you have passion.
Write down what's stopping you, develop a proactive plan, act, and move ahead.

> "The way to get started is to quit talking and begin doing."
> —Walt Disney
>
> "The beginning is the most important part of the work." —Plato
>
> "There comes a time when the risk to remain tight in the bud is more painful than the risk it takes to blossom." —Anais Nin

Overcome Your Obstacles

> "If you find a path with no obstacles, it probably doesn't lead anywhere."
> —Frank A. Clark

Stay Motivated

You can't run away from a challenge, run toward it.

> "People often say that motivation doesn't last. Well neither does bathing that's why we recommend it daily."
> —Zig Ziglar

> "The sun will rise and set regardless. What we choose to do with the light while it's here is up to us."
> —Alexandra Elle

Be Committed

> "Wheresoever you go, go with all your heart."
> —Confucius

> "You can neither win nor lose if you don't run the race."
> —David Bowie

Be Reflective

Question your motivations and priorities.
Ensure you are being true to what really matters to you.

> "Never work just for power or money. They won't save your soul or help you sleep at night."
> —Marian Wright Edelman

> "You are the window through which you must see the world."
> —George Bernard Shaw

> "It is not the mountain we conquer but ourselves."
> —Sir Edmund Hillary

Ensure Your Work Has Meaning

> "Never doubt that a small group of thoughtful committed people can change the world. Indeed, it is the only thing that ever has."
> —Margaret Mead

Enjoy **the Climb**

Make it fun.
The view is interesting all the way up.
And there is a lot to learn at every level.

> *"If the path be beautiful, let us not ask where it leads."*
> —Anatole France
>
> *"Adopt the pace of nature. Her secret is patience."*
> —Ralph Waldo Emerson
>
> *"Have patience with all things. But, first of all yourself."*
> —Saint Francis de Sales

Enjoy the Ride

"It does not matter how slow you go, as long as you do not stop."
—Confucius

"Write it on your heart that every day is the best day of the year."
—Ralph Waldo Emerson

"Life is a journey, not a destination."
—Ralph Waldo Emerson

"It is good to have an end to journey toward, but it is the journey that matters in the end."
—Ursula K. Le Guin

"Success usually comes to those too busy to be looking for it."
—Henry David Thoreau

"Whatever you are, be a good one."
—Abraham Lincoln

"Put your heart, mind, and soul into even your smallest acts. This is the secret to success."
—Swami Sivananda

Appreciate **the** Magic **in Today**

Be present in each moment.
Enjoy today while you build toward tomorrow.

"True happiness is to enjoy the present without anxious dependence upon the future." —Lucius Seneca

• • •

"One's destination is never a place, but a new way of seeing things." —Henry Miller

• • •

"Joy is what happens to us when we recognize how good things really are." —Marianne Williamson

• • •

"We travel the world over in search of what we need and return home to find it." —George Moore

• • •

"Now and then it's good to pause in our pursuit of happiness, and just be happy." —Guillaume Apollinaire

• • •

"The future depends on what you do today." —Gandhi

• • •

"It's not always that we need to do more but rather we need to focus on less." —Nathan W. Morris

• • •

"The simplest questions are often the most profound. What are you doing? Where are you going?" —Richard Bach

---

Exercise #6

Proactive Prioritization and Your Daily Three MUST DO's

● ● ●

We all have "to-do" lists, whether in our head or written down. Most of these good-intentioned lists are fully overwhelming—maybe even humanly impossible to achieve.

Keeping with our simple, yet significant and strategic theme, try prioritizing just three tasks each day and make a full commitment to those. Simply agree with yourself that your day is not over until you have completed these three activities in full. New rule: you must do your three Must Do's.

Consider giving yourself a variety of priorities and of course ensure they align with your short and long-term goals.

Here are a few ideas for how to vary and categorize your three priorities:

Positivity, Relationship, and Motivation.

Personal, Professional, and Philanthropic.

Low Hanging Fruit, Stretch Goal, and Serious Game Changer.

Health, Wealth, and Wisdom.

Me, Family, and Others.

Easy, Challenging, and Scary.

Whatever parameters you choose for your daily three Must Do's, ensure they are ambitious, yet feasible and close to your heart.

So what three priorities will you commit to today knowing that you are in the driver's seat of each day? You and only you are singularly accountable for your day, your destiny, and your legacy.

My Must Do list for today is:

1. I must_____

_____

2. I must_____

_____

3. I must_____

_____

Chapter 7
Summing Up Your
Happily Ever After Plan

Crap We Can't Control

We didn't spend a lot of time on the crap you can't control. Hard core truth; bad things happen even at the supposed happiest place on earth. Disney has challenging internal politics, periods of declining box office, theme park attendance, and product sales. The most important message here is to learn from it. Everything does happen for a reason and usually it's a lesson and a blessing in disguise. There are hidden treasures in the challenges. And you *can* control how you will react, respond, and learn from obstacles you must leap over on your path.

"Strength does not come from physical capacity. It comes from an indomitable will."　　　　　　　　　　　　　—Gandhi

"Running away from any problem only increases the distance from the solution. The easiest way to escape the problem is to solve it."　　　　　　　　　　　　　—Unknown

Injustice Happens

You will likely experience someone else getting a promotion or recognition you should have gotten. The odds are you will likely get laid off at least once and it could be for reasons completely out of your control. Don't be bitter and angry. Really ask yourself is there anything I could have done differently? More importantly, what can I do now? Learn. Ask for input. Make any needed improvements. Then go for your wildest dreams again! And this time, aim even higher.

"The flower that blooms in adversity is the most rare and beautiful of all." —The Emperor of China, from the movie *Mulan*

Companies Do Not Hug Back

Any time you start to feel resentment toward your work, stop. Take a moment to consider what you are sacrificing—your workout, your family, or a hobby which fuels your energy. Seek balance. You are going to be better at your job if you are happy from the inside out. We cannot fake these things. Commit to balance no matter what. It is the quality you bring to your job and not the quantity. Do not work more than your mind and heart can handle.

"Next to love, balance is the most important thing." —John Wooden

"The purpose of our lives is to be happy." —Dalai Lama

"Happiness is not by chance, but by choice." —Jim Rohn

"Some of us think holding on makes us strong but sometimes it is letting go." —Hermann Hesse

Did I Forget to Talk About Money?

Nope. I didn't forget. I seriously just didn't think of it much during my career or when recounting some of my most important lessons and best memories. It really was never about the money during my entire career. Based on my experience, and watching the careers of many others, if you take care of your relationships, stay positive no matter what, and are self-motivated, the money will follow.

Crap We Can Control

You, and only you, are in control of your destiny and your happiness.

The secret to your success and your happiness is all up to you. Do not expect anyone to be more important than you are as you go forward! You have to believe in yourself. You have to manage your personal style and ensure your energy is always solution oriented and positive. You need to give back to and rally your relationships. You have to wake up ready to make the most of every day. You have to know your strengths and know that *you* are the only thing standing in the way of your full potential—whether it be self-doubt, fear of failure, fear of success or anger . . . identify these blind spots proactively so you can control them and push forward.

Believe!

Be the best you all the time . . . no matter what!

Think about whom you would count on first in a crisis. Who would you want holding your hand when you are down? Who would you want to hang out with at a party? Who would you want leading you in times of challenge or great opportunity? And then just model that person! Don't let anyone or any situation impact you to the point that you disappoint yourself. Be a person you admire, trust, and respect. Compete with yourself. Be the best you. Be the you that you dreamed of being when you were five years old. Believe in yourself and cheer for yourself with unwavering enthusiasm.

"Believe you can and you're half way there." —Theodore Roosevelt

"Optimism is an intellectual choice." —Diana Schneider

"Nothing reduces the odds against you like ignoring them." —Robert Brault

"Magic is believing in yourself. If you can do that you can make anything happen." —Goethe

Take Action!

Prioritize faith, love, and people—at work and in life

Don't climb your way up the ladder and find out you are alone when you get there. Your computer may know all your secrets and make you laugh, but just like your company, it can't hug you back. Look at the faces and gifts of family and friendship around you. Focus on the people at work. Focus on the people important to you in your life. In the end, we all want the same thing: to love and to be loved. It is so simple; it's sometimes hard to see or believe that it all boils down to love and following what is in our hearts.

"The most important things in life aren't things." —Anthony J. D'Angelo

"For small creatures such as we, the vastness is bearable only through love." —Carl Sagan

> *"Faith makes all things possible. Love makes all things easy."*
> —Dwight L. Moody
>
> *"Work to become, not to acquire."* —Elbert Hubbard
>
> *"Strive not to be a success, but rather of value."* —Albert Einstein
>
> *"When you arise in the morning, think of what a precious privilege it is to be alive—to breathe, to think, to enjoy, and to live."*
> —Marcus Aurelius

Be your own top competitor and unwavering champion.
Challenge yourself, cheer for yourself and fearlessly go for your wildest dreams.

> *"Whatever you are ready for is ready for you."*—Mark Victor Hansen

Love yourself. Love those around you. Be generous. Be grateful. Believe. Your happily ever after is fully in your control. Take charge. Do this and strive for inner peace. Ensure what you are doing has meaning to you. Don't forget your RPMs. Prioritize your Relationships, your Positivity, and your own Motivation. When you do, your success and your full happiness are guaranteed. Enjoy your happily ever after.

> *"The love we give away is the only love we keep."*—Elbert Hubbard
>
> *"Our truest life is when we are in dreams awake."*
> —Henry David Thoreau
>
> *"One day your life will pass before your eyes. Make sure it is worth watching."*
> —Gerard Way

Now Is a Good Time to Start

> *"Don't wait. The time will never be just right."* —Napoleon Hill
>
> *"The beginning is the most important part of the work."* —Plato

Aim High

"In the long run, you hit what you aim at, so aim high."
—Henry David Thoreau

• • •

"Reach high, for the stars lie hidden in your soul. Dream deep, for every dream precedes the goal."
—Pamela Vaull Starr

• • •

"Risk more than others think is safe. Care more than others think is wise. Dream more than others think is practical. Expect more than others think is possible."
—Cadet Maxim

• • •

"To do the useful thing, to say the courageous thing, to contemplate the beautiful thing, that is enough for one man's life."
—T. S. Eliot

• • •

"The more you are motivated by love, the more fearless and free your actions will be."
—Dalai Lama

• • •

"Enjoy the little things in life because one day you'll look back and realize they were the big things."
—Kurt Vonnegut

• • •

"Never give up. And never under any circumstances, face the facts."
—Ruth Gordon

• • •

"It is precisely the possibility of realizing a dream that makes life interesting."
—Paulo Coelho

• • •

"Every great dream begins with a dreamer. Always remember, you have within you the strength, the patience, and the passion to reach for the stars, to change the world."
—Harriet Tubman

• • •

"The essentials of happiness are: something to do, something to love, and something to hope for."
—Allan K. Chalmers

YOUR KEYS TO HAPPILY EVER AFTER
Top Ten Tip List
Relationships, Positivity, and Motivation
(RPMs)

1. Bring your heart to work.
2. Prioritize people and pets.
3. Treat everyone equally with kindness.
4. Laugh and make the work fun.
5. Be positive no matter what.
6. Be slow to panic—maintain perspective.
7. Know it is all up to you; motivate yourself.
8. Say it out loud and believe.
9. Dream, aim high and take action.
10. Keep moving forward; never give up!

Exercise #7

My Happily Ever After Plan

Starting today, I am going to do the following ten things consistently to show up as my best self, to keep my relationships thriving and to motivate myself to keep moving toward my largest goals in life.

1. _____

2. _____

3. _____

4. _____

5. _____

6. _____

7. _____

8. _____

9. _____

10. _____